THE PICTORIAL HISTORY OF SEA BATTLES

THOMAS FOSTER

ENIGMA

SEA BATTLES

PICTURES SUPPLIED BY:

Camera Press Ltd. 71, 79, 100, 102
The County Studio 8, 16, 36, 48, 76, 84, 102, 108, 120
Fujifotos 58, 59, 60, 63, 64
Sonia Halliday 17
Imperial War Museum 4, 70, 74, 78, 82, 86, 87, 90, 94, 95, 98, 101, 105, 106, 110, 112, 113, 114
Imperial War/Museum Chris Barker 72-73
Mansell Collection 6, 7, 10, 11, 12, 14, 18, 24, 31, 44, 46
J. G. Moore Collection 38, 71
National Maritime Museum, London 20, 26, 28, 30, 40, 44, 52, 92
National Maritime Museum, London/ Chris Barker 34
Dudley Pope 50
P & O Steamship Company 86, 88-89
Ullstein GmbH Front Cover
US Navy ,Washington 116, 118, 123, 124, 126, 128
Victoria & Albert Museum 68
Ray Woodward/Blandford Press Ltd. 22, 32, 42, 81, 96

Maps by Roger Kelly

Published by Enigma Books Limited,
58 Old Compton Street, London W1V 5PA

© Marshall Cavendish Limited 1974, 1977

First printing 1974
Second printing 1977

Printed in Hong Kong

ISBN 0 85685 077 2

ABOUT THIS BOOK

Here is the book that covers every aspect of that
vast subject—war at sea.

From Nelson's bravery at Cape St Vincent
to the death of the *Bismarck*, the pride of
Hitler's Navy, from galleys rowed by slaves to the
battleships and aircraft carriers the USA
and Japan threw against each other in
World War II, from the 32-pounder cannon
to the 16-inch guns at Jutland.
The Pictorial History of Sea Battles
is the story of conflict at sea.

The authoritative and highly-readable text
has all the information you require,
specially-drawn maps give you a clear guide
to the action, detailed diagrams flesh out the
technical specifications of ships and guns and
dozens of illustrations, many in full colour,
bring you the excitement, the danger—and
the sadness—of war.

The Pictorial History of Sea Battles
will take you right into the world of the great
admirals, the great heroes and the great fighting
ships. Once it is on your bookshelf you will
consult it again and again.

CONTENTS

SALAMIS

Galleys against galleys, mighty empire against city state — and victory went to the 'weaker' side. At Salamis on the Aegean Sea in 480 B.C., the vast and unwieldy Persian armada was beaten by half the number of sleek and better-crewed Greek Triremes.

'Master, remember the Athenians . . . remember the Athenians' whispered the slave. His master was Xerxes, the warrior king of the Persian Empire and he had good cause to remember the Greeks. Years earlier the forces of the young and ambitious Persian Empire, under Xerxes's father Darius, had been smashed by the Athenians on the plains of Marathon. Xerxes was determined to gain revenge—and this led to one of the greatest sea battles in history, at Salamis in 480 B.C.

In two areas of the Mediterranean, then the centre of the known world, two young empires, the Greek and the Persian, were growing and spreading their influence. Greece possessed the most enlightened and free society of the ancient world and this was pitted against the expanding empire of the despotic Persians.

The seeds of war

Conflict between the two empires had started in a small way with fighting in the border towns of Greece and Persia. Persia was here flexing her muscles and trying her strength but as the years passed the fighting increased in ferocity, first on land, then on the sea. At times it appeared as if the fate of the whole of the then known world hung on the outcome of these small and petty battles.

The first recorded battle between the two empires was in the first half of the seventh century B.C., when the Persians attacked some

Top *Themistocles personified the vigorous Athenian spirit. He realized that Greek freedom depended on sea power and so persuaded the Athenians to expand the navy and train seamen.*

Below *Xerxes thought Greece would fall without struggle to the juggernaut of the Persian army and his ships were built to carry the maximum number of soldiers rather than for battle at sea.*

Left *When the two fleets met at Salamis, Themistocles' foresight paid off – and the Greeks, although heavily outnumbered, drove off the Persians.*

Greek cities on the border. The Greeks were quick to reply and, of course, the Persians replied again. Attacks and counter-attacks continued sporadically for the next few centuries. In the year 494 B.C., the Persians attacked Miletus and razed it to the ground. This was a terrible blow to the Greeks, for Miletus had been the richest and most brilliant of all the Ionian cities. The Athenian poet, Phrynichus, wrote the story of this tragedy—his play *The Capture of Miletus* was so overwhelming that the Athenian audience was moved to tears and wailing. Phrynichus was duly fined 1,000 drachmas for depressing his audience!

In the years that followed the Persians systematically nibbled at the borders of the Grecian Empire. City after city fell into Persian hands as they slowly got the better of their Greek adversaries. This could not continue much longer—if it did Greece would surely slip

Good training and highly-manoeuvrable ships were the key to Greek success at Salamis. Their fast-moving Triremes **left,** *driven by 170 slaves pulling on oars up to 14 feet long, were armed with metal-tipped, trident-shaped rams that ripped the Persian galleys apart. The much heavier Persian* Trieres *were really troop-carriers: although propelled by 200 oarsmen, they could not escape the darting Greek ships.*

under Persian domination. Then came the battle of Marathon.

Darius strikes at Greece

In the year 490 B.C., Darius I, who had succeeded to the Persian throne, struck at the Grecian Empire once more. A fleet of 600 ships sailed across the Aegean Sea towards the Bay of

Marathon. The Persians planned to land troops there to march on Athens and overrun it before the Greeks could muster any effective resistance. But the Persians sailed off course and had to revise their strategy. Their new plan was to sail round and attack Athens through the port of Phaleron. This manoeuvre took time though and the Athenians had warning of attack. In a hurried last minute plan they decided on their tactics.

The Persian and Greek armies met on the plains of Marathon. The Persians reeled under the violent Greek onslaught. The wings of the Greek army crushed their opposing forces and, wheeling inwards towards the centre, butchered the remaining troops. The Persians' army collapsed in disarray, huge numbers being slain or driven into the sea. A few fought a rearguard action and escaped in their ships but when the clamour

of battle died the grim toll was known—6,400 crack troops from the Persian army killed against the Greek loss of just 192 soldiers. Today the plain of Marathon has a high mound in the middle and legend tells that this is the spot where the ashes of the Greek dead were buried.

After the crushing victory of Marathon the Greeks had some ten years of respite. The Persians spent this time licking their wounds. Xerxes, the son of Darius, succeeded him to the throne of Persia in the year 485 B.C.

Xerxes avenges Marathon

Xerxes was determined to avenge the bitter ignominy of Marathon and prepared to strike at the Greeks once more. He gathered forces from far and wide, from India, Egypt, even Ethiopia and planned and trained a massive army. He also built the greatest battle fleet the world had ever seen. Persian pride demanded that the failure at Marathon must be erased from the minds of Persians.

Below This carving of a Greek Trireme *shows the three banks of sweeps that propelled the ship. Most of the oars were pulled by two men, some by three.*

Opposite It was the desire to revenge the earlier Greek victory on the plains of Marathon that led Xerxes to strike at the Greeks once more.

While Xerxes was planning the downfall of the Greek empire, the Athenians had been embroiled in internal political and military squabbles that could only weaken them in the face of a fresh Persian onslaught. Then one man, Themistocles, came to the forefront. Themistocles, in the coming years, was to personify the vigorous Athenian spirit of freewill. He was an impetuous man but a quick learner who became a very gifted politician with great foresight, for he alone realized that the future of Athens lay not in protecting its vast boundaries, but in sea power. Athens would flower only if the sea lanes were kept open and free from Persian aggression: Athens would wither and die if the Persians gained a strangle-hold on those sea lanes. This was Themistocles' simple, direct, reasoning.

So, in 483 B.C., Themistocles persuaded the Athenian Assembly to expand its navy. The old ships were replaced by warships of the latest design; men were trained and retrained in the arts of seaborne warfare; navigation, strategy, weaponry and all the other arts of war were drilled into the fighting men of Athens.

Three years after the Athenians had started to expand their navy Xerxes had completed the ten year task of building a mighty Persian force to do battle with the Greeks. The Persians now had a huge army of over two million men, 1,200 warships and 3,000 smaller vessels. A formidable force of disciplined warriors was now at Xerxes' command. The day was drawing near when he would seek vengeance for the humiliation of Marathon.

Three hundred Immortals

In 480 B.C., Xerxes moved against the Grecian Empire. Athens, thanks to Themistocles, was now far better prepared than she had ever been for the oncoming crisis. The Greeks had called on their allies and the Spartans, renowned for their brave and disciplined military prowess, now led the Greek army. Calling the combined military force *The League of the Greeks*, the Spartans massed the troops on the northern border near the narrow pass at Thermopylae. To attack Athens, Xerxes must lead his army through this pass.

Although the forces of the Persian empire suffered losses in a storm when several convoy supply ships grounded, the great juggernaut advanced, slowly but relentlessly and soon the Persian army was at the approaches to Thermopylae—once through the pass Athens, the centre of Greek culture, stood before them. But the narrow pass was now defended by a tiny but dedicated group of Spartan soldiers, remembered for their heroism as the 'Immortal 300'. The Greek defence held out against the huge power of Xerxes' army and gave Themistocles the breathing space he needed to organize the Greek fleet into battle stations. Thermopylae fell—but not before the gallant stand of the Immortal 300 had won valuable time for the Greeks.

After the fall of Thermopylae, the city of Athens was evacuated in preparation for the coming invasion. Themistocles ordered the women and children to the outlying cities of Salamis, Troezen and Aegina for safety. He then recruited all the remaining able-bodied men to fortify the Greek navy and set about the difficult tactical task of ensuring that the Greek navy went into combat with the Persian fleet on its own terms.

THE BATTLE OF MARATHON.

While Xerxes led his army forward from Thermopylae and into the empty city of Athens Themistocles finally shaped his tactics into a plan based on one very simple requirement—the Persian fleet had to be met in a restricted sea. So long as the battle was fought in a sea full of uncharted dangers and limited in space to

manoeuvre, the superior seamanship of the Greeks, rather than numbers, would win the day.

So with this plan in mind Themistocles regrouped his fleet at Salamis ready to fight in the narrow channel between the island of Salamis and the mainland, not far from Athens. If the Persian fleet could be destroyed here Xerxes would be forced to retire from the city, his lines of supply and communication cut.

Battering rams versus . . .

Slowly the Greek fleet grouped itself. The spearheads of the Greek navy were *Triremes*, oar-driven timber warships, rowed into battle by 170 selected oarsmen. The ships were stoutly built with narrow hulls and streamlined looks which presented a very low profile in the water. The prow, designed for ramming, was built forward and outward as a battering ram with a metal cap shaped like a trident, the weapon of the Sea God, Poseidon. A trireme could be manoeuvred quickly and skilfully into battle positions and the oarsmen could propel the ship forward at high speed to crush anything in its path. Archers

Above The unwieldy Persian galleys could not manoeuvre in the dangerous waters and many ran aground – or even smashed into each other.

Right Choosing the narrow channel at Salamis as the battle ground gave Themistocles and the light Greek ships the advantage they needed.

stood on the prow of each warship and from there rained down arrows into the enemies' ships. Themistocles had over 200 of these finely built, extremely efficient, 'battering ram' warships under his command.

. . . lumbering hulks

Xerxes' fleet, on the other hand, was not designed for combat at sea but for landing and boarding tactics, and for bringing ashore vast quantities of troops and munitions. The Persian warships, *Trieres*, were mighty looking vessels between 120 and 140 feet long. They rode high in the water and carried a towering stern and lofty decks, under which vast quantities of munitions,

Salamis

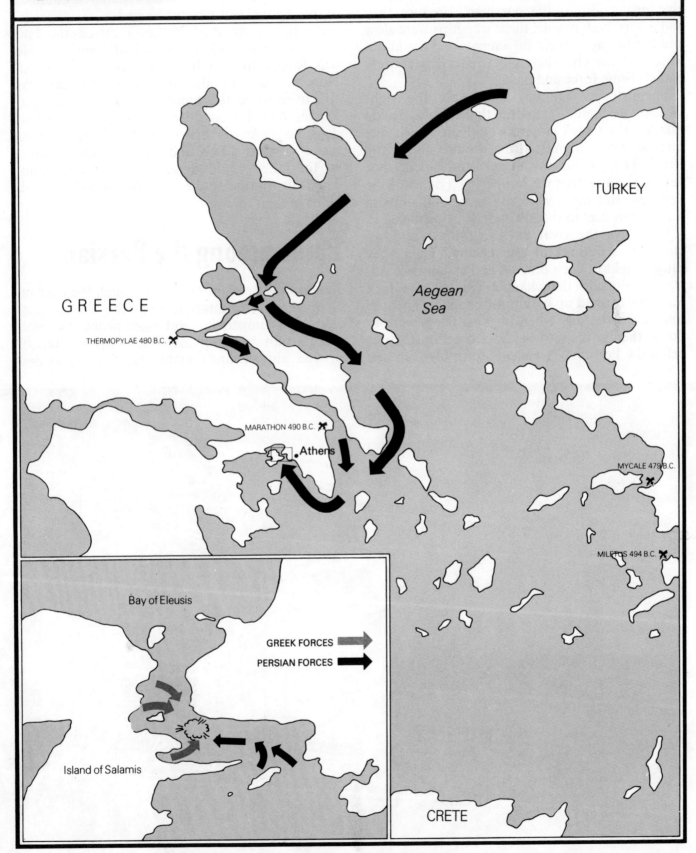

TURKEY

GREECE

Aegean Sea

THERMOPYLAE 480 B.C.

MARATHON 490 B.C.

Athens

MYCALE 479 B.C.

MILETUS 494 B.C.

Bay of Eleusis

GREEK FORCES

PERSIAN FORCES

Island of Salamis

CRETE

stores and marine soldiers could be kept. They were particularly noticeable, for, unlike the Greek warships, they carried rows of the marine soldiers' shields down the sides of the ship to give protection to the oarsmen. Because they had a very high profile, these warships were slow and lumbering in their movements and could not be turned quickly. Their effectiveness lay entirely in their brute force and power.

Themistocles had chosen exactly the right location to fight the battle that would decide whether the Greek empire would survive or die. The narrow Salamis strait would allow the Greek Triremes to move freely and quickly but hamper and restrict the lumbering Trieres of the Persians. But there were still some 800 ships in the Persian fleet to the 200 under Themistocles.

For days the rival navies grouped and re-grouped, scouting for the enemy. Then they caught sight of each other. The Persian fleet was massed outside the channel while the Greek warships formed up within the channel. Then, at sunrise on the day when the two fleets were to throw themselves into battle, a cruel misfortune befell the Persians. A violent storm blew up and

sent many of the Persian ships, which were on the open sea and unsheltered, crashing on to the rocks. The Persian fleet was badly mauled—the Greek fleet, in the narrow and sheltered confines of the channel was barely touched.

As the storm died Xerxes received the bad news—over half of his ships had been lost. He was forced to withdraw his ships to regroup. Now he had just under 400 ships left but this was still over twice the number in the Greek fleet. Xerxes was still confident of victory. After two days he gave the order for his battle-fleet to move forward slowly and crush the Greek ships so that they could drive straight on to land. Then his marine soldiers would have the Greek lands at their mercy.

Panic among the Persians

Xerxes now brought his fleet through the narrow channel ready to smash through the 'lightweight' ships of Themistocles. But more problems befell the Persian battle plans. The narrow channel proved almost unnavigable for the high-sided

Persian warships. Lumbering out of line, they impeded each other. The Persian sailors started to panic and the loss of proper command spread throughout the Persian fleet. Xerxes now realized that the ships could not, in these conditions, navigate with the degree of accuracy that he wanted.

At this moment, while the commanders of the Persian warships were concentrating all their powers on navigating through the dangerously narrow waters, Themistocles struck. The Greek ships, fewer in number but far better manoeuvred and managed, moved easily through the narrow waters. Darting amongst the clumsy Persian warships, harrying them, driving them into each other, battering them with their massive rams the Greek Triremes wrought havoc. Persian warship after Persian warship foundered, crushed under the onslaught of the darting, ever-present Greek ships. Xerxes' mighty vessels collapsed like matchwood under the impact of the 'trident' rams. Their commanders were in complete disarray, unable to navigate the treacherous waters and unable to turn quickly. Their ships ran aground or smashed against the shallow reefs. Amid all the chaos, a relentless hail of arrows from the Greek archers rained down on the Persian warships.

The sea gives up its dead

Ship after ship turned over, foundered or ran aground. The sea changed colour from limpid blue to dark red as the waters ran thick with Persian blood. Trieres were crushed between land and battering ram. The marine soldiers, weighed down by their shields and armour, drowned without a hope of making the shore and without getting to grips with the enemy. Time and time again Themistocles regrouped his ships to drive them forward into the now completely disordered Persian navy. The sea became choked with the wreckage of ships and the bodies of slaughtered men. The straggling Persian ships, as they tried desperately and clumsily to turn about and make for the open sea, managed only to ram each other.

For 12 hours the Greek ships battered the Persian galleys, sinking more than 200 and turning the seas red with blood, until the Persians fled.

The blood-bath continued for over 12 hours. Xerxes had made a tragic mistake by trying to fight a battle on terms dictated by Themistocles. In the confined channel at Salamis the advantage had always been with the faster, lighter ships of the Greek navy. As the grey light of dusk closed in eye witnesses saw the Greek coast piled high with the carnage from the battle. The sea had returned the dead to the land, a land that for thousands of Persians once seemed to offer plunder and riches and now afforded only an unfriendly grave.

During the evening and the early hours of the morning the Greek ships withdrew to harbour, the warriors exultant in victory. The remains of Xerxes' Persian fleet limped into open waters to assess the damage. Exhausted, they counted their losses—of the 400 ships that had sailed proudly into battle at dawn, 200 had not returned. Half the battle fleet was lost. The Persians knew they could not continue the battle but more than that, they resolved, after the vicious defeat in the narrow channel of Salamis, never to send their ships against the Greek fleet again. Persian pride, bolstered during the long years waiting to avenge Marathon, had been crushed and their warrior king, Xerxes, went home defeated. He withdrew from Athens as Themistocles had expected, taking his troops and the remainder of his navy with him. The bloody battle was at an end.

By any standards the Greek victory at Salamis was an astonishing achievement. In view of the odds they overcame, the Greeks were rightfully filled with self-confidence, patriotism and pride and dramatists and poets recorded the noble deeds of Salamis.

Freedom!

After further years of small skirmishes on the borders, the Persians, now without a navy, and with a much depleted army, settled for a treaty of peace. This treaty recognized the liberty of the Greek states in Europe and Asia. The mighty sea battle of Salamis guaranteed the survival of the cultured Athenian state and crushed the ambitions of the autocratic Persian empire. The freedom of the individual in the most enlightened of all ancient empires had been safeguarded against the threat of harsh, unbending Persian rule and Greece lived on to deepen its influence on the civilization that followed it.

PREVEZA

At Preveza on the Ionian Sea in 1537, the ex-pirate Barbarossa drove his Turkish galleys against the Spanish galleons of Andrea Doria. After a day of cannon salvos, ramming and hand-to-hand-fighting. Doria fled, leaving Barbarossa 'King of the Seas'.

A pirate, known by friends and enemies alike as 'Redbeard' or Barbarossa, plied the Eastern waters of the Mediterranean in the early years of the sixteenth century. From very humble beginnings Barbarossa, together with his two brothers, rose from strength to strength. By example, courage and skulduggery this Barbary pirate, Khair-ed-Din Barbarossa, rose in stature in the eyes of the Sultan of the Ottoman Empire until, by the year 1533, he became, by the Sultan's command, the Grand Admiral of the Turkish Fleet.

Grand Admiral Khair-ed-Din Barbarossa proved himself to be a natural leader of the Ottoman Navy. At its helm he steered the Ottoman Empire into a massive Turkish-Ottoman alliance. He alone was mainly responsible for the upsurge of the Turkish and Moslem influence throughout the first half of the sixteenth century, an influence that slowly but surely spread across the Mediterranean.

In Barbarossa's Turkish Navy, slaves rowed galleys up to 150 feet long into action. The Spanish had huge sailing galleons as well as galleys – but these were a liability despite their heavy artillery. Unable to keep formation or make headway in light winds they fell easy prey to Barbarossa's oar-driven warships.

Barbarossa rose from Barbary pirate to Grand Admiral of the Turkish Fleet, but drew upon his pirate experience in defeating the Spanish Fleet at Preveza. He died in 1546, one of the major figures of the Ottoman empire.

Khair-ed-Din Barbarossa rapidly gained a reputation as the 'King' of the seas, the greatest Admiral that the Turks had ever known. He put the years of experience gained from piracy to good use and controlled the Eastern Mediterranean with a firm, but skilful, hand from his base at Constantinople.

The chief opponent of the increasing Moslem infiltration was Catholic Spain and the Spanish fought and fought again, in skirmishes and running fights, throughout the length and breadth of the Mediterranean, against the spread of what was to them the 'heathen' influence of the Ottoman Empire.

Spain, wishing to make alliances to combat the advance of their religious enemies courted the Italian states and Rome, the seat of the Catholic Empire. The courting proved successful and old and often bitter differences were forgotten in the common religious cause. An alliance was forged so that Spain might not only protect herself but also start to win back the sea power that she had already lost to the Turks. It was, or was called, a holy cause.

Spanish raids

The clash between Moslem Ottoman Empire and Catholic Spain came at last when the Spanish fleet, under the Genoese Admiral Andrea Doria, began the fight back. The religious war had started. The opening round was a Spanish raid which took the Turkish outpost of Coron, in Morea, in the southern part of Greece.

Barbarossa was perturbed for his plan for complete domination of the Mediterranean under the Moslem religion was under attack. He knew

he would have to confront the Spanish – and win. Slowly and steadily he devised the strategy and tactics that would bring victory.

One year and then two slipped by and still Barbarossa planned. He was loathe to move his complete navy, so, in the meantime, he maintained a policy of small violent confrontations at the outposts of the Empire. While these small engagements went on he designed plans for the greater kill.

By 1537 Barbarossa's plans were ready. His fleet, sailing from Constantinople, swept into the open Mediterranean. Coastal towns along the 'toe' of Italy were besieged while Barbarossa's ships played havoc with any Spanish or Italian craft that might fall into his path. The bait was being laid.

Week after week violent raids were carried out against outposts of the Catholic alliance. The raids continued throughout the summer. Would these skirmishes against the smaller fish entice the bigger fish? Barbarossa waited: then the news came. Andrea Doria had gathered together a massive fleet – the bait had been taken up.

Barbarossa's trap

Barbarossa's plans now began to unfold – the 'holy' battle was about to begin. He took his fleet through the winding channels of the many islands of southern Greece, into the Gulf of Arta. Here his fleet could lie in wait, in sheltered safety. He brought his fleet into a huge quadrant with the bows of the ships pointing towards the narrow entrance of the gulf. If Andrea Doria followed he would fall into a trap. Barbarossa, using his vast knowledge obtained by years of piracy, had chosen this anchorage with care – here he could do battle on his own terms.

Andrea Doria, unaware of the exact whereabouts of Barbarossa, brought his fleet into the Turkish-dominated waters and began to search. Through the early part of September, Andrea Doria hunted the Turkish Admiral and his fleet and then on finding him realized he would have to take the Gulf of Arta and flush out the enemy. But the channel leading into the Gulf was narrow and treacherous and the task would not be easy.

On September 25, the Spanish fleet lay off the entrance to the channel. The fleet, a mixture of oar-driven galleys and sailing galleons, vastly outnumbered the Turkish Navy, and Andrea

Doria thought that by sheer weight of numbers he could overwhelm Barbarossa's fleet.

But Barbarossa knew better. The heavier ships, the galleons, of the Spanish could navigate the channel only one at a time and as his fleet covered the entrance to the channel he could literally pick them off one at a time before they could take up battle formations. His light but extremely well-equipped galleys could fly forward and ram the massive Papal galleons as they spilled out through the channel.

Doria knew, as only an experienced Admiral could know, that under these conditions he could not hope for victory – his towering galleons could not safely navigate the channel. So he waited. The two navies were at either end of a long, tortuous and dangerous channel, each waiting for the other to venture through. Of the two positions, Barbarossa's was the happier in an enclosed gulf protected from the violent squalls prevalent at that time of year. Doria's fleet on the other hand, was exposed and a sudden squall would give him little time to seek shelter.

First blood

This appeared to favour Barbarossa – but he realized a potential danger. Doria, with his superior manpower, might seek to land his troops and his cannons, force-march them over the isthmus and lay seige to Barbarossa's fleet. If he did he could fire down at will upon the Turks and slowly bring their fleet to submission. But it was Barbarossa not Doria, who made the first move.

Taking the initiative, Barbarossa landed some soldiers and drove them hard over the isthmus with orders to set up a battery to bombard the enemy's fleet. But Doria spotted movement high on the shoreline and he brought his massive galleons as close as he dared to the shore. The Spanish gunners took steady aim and blasted Barbarossa's men before they had time to establish themselves. The cannons of the huge galleons ripped into the shoreline. Men fell

Opposite The Spanish Fleet had galleys as well as galleons and these too carried heavy artillery.

Right Andrea Doria, 1466–1560, was a great 'Freelance' admiral. Genoese by birth, he fought for several masters, usually with great success. Some rumours suggested he lost the battle of Preveza on purpose – because his fees had not been paid!

Overleaf The Battle of Lepanto in 1571 involved virtually the same forces as fought at Preveza. But Barbarossa and Doria were both dead and victory this time went to the Christian alliance.

without having the chance to reply and the rest fled in disarray. The short violent action ended when Andrea Doria withdrew his ships to deeper water, leaving Barbarossa's men to march their way back across the isthmus. Of those that had set out, less than half returned. Barbarossa had not yet fired a shot – and he had lost valuable men and armaments.

The quiet stalemate resumed, a cat and mouse game between two fleets. Then, after days of waiting, the Genoese Admiral made a move. He withdrew his fleet and headed south for the comparative shelter of the island of Levkas. His aim was to tempt Barbarossa into pursuit, out of the Gulf of Arta – would it work?

On the morning of September 27, Barbarossa responded as Doria had hoped. The Turkish

A Spanish galleass carried soldiers as well as sailors for boarding parties and hand-to-hand fighting. The broadside guns were mounted below the tiers of oars, which had to be raised so that the galleass could fire without crippling herself.

Admiral brought his fleet from their safe anchorage, through the narrow channel and out into open water. Driving his galleys as fast as he could he chased the fleeing Papal Fleet.

Andrea Doria was still trying to bring his massive fleet of many hundreds of royal and golden galleys and galleons into formation. At first the massive galleons under their huge canvasses appeared to come into position, but then the fickle wind dropped, leaving the canvasses hanging limply. Slaves, pulling at lengthy oars, tried to row the cumbersome galleys into formation but with scant success – the Papal fleet lost all coordination.

Into battle

Andrea Doria's fleet was strung out into a long, disorganized line – the Spanish Admiral could not afford to meet Barbarossa in this position. But to his dismay Barbarossa's fleet appeared over the

horizon. In perfect formation, the galleys, their blades flashing in the sun, bore down on the ragged line of the Papal fleet. The towering royal galleons of Spain could make little headway or escape from the powerful oar-driven warships. Barbarossa, in the leading galley, ploughed into the tail end of the straggling line while the galleons of the Spanish were almost unable to move forward.

The first shots rang out and cannons opened fire between the two closing enemies. Wave after wave of piercing attacks struck the straggling line of Doria's fleet. Driving the galleys on with every ounce of strength, the Turks slammed into the sides of the Spanish ships. With great crashing of timbers the galleons reeled under the impact as the Turkish galleys rammed, butted and bruised their way into the heart of the straggling fleet. The Papal ships fought back, blasting salvo after salvo into the waves of approaching galleys. Their cannons ripped gaping holes in the Turkish warships, smashing oars and men alike. The sides of the galleys were stove in and the oars, splintered and broken, fell from lifeless hands. Death and destruction were heaped on the heads of the galley slaves, as they strove to drive their ships onward, into the sides of the galleons.

The first attack was beaten off and the galleys withdrew. Barbarossa had suffered terrible losses, but had inflicted much damage. Ruined and wrecked ships littered the sea for the short violent action had ended with many hundreds of casualties on both sides. Barbarossa watched as his galleys limped back and regrouped. One of them, unable to bear its wounds any longer, slipped under the waves, taking with it screaming sailors and slaves.

A breathing space

The advantage was now with the Genoese Admiral. He ordered his guns to fire at will at the straggling galleys as they attempted to regroup and sweep forward into another attack. Andrea Doria ordered his ships to move in, do as much damage as they could in as short a time as possible and then withdraw before the Turks could respond. But the fickle winds made this manoeuvre impossible. Barbarossa was given a precious breathing space. His galleys regrouped and like angry hornets darted forward to deliver their sting.

The battle raged all day. Up and down the coastline the violent action raged until well into the afternoon. The light wind at last rose, filling the sails of the great Papal galleons, and Andrea Doria's fleet withdrew in a now fairly ordered formation, leaving Barbarossa's fleet to follow at will.

The 'pirate' Admiral would not allow the enemy to slip from his grasp so easily and he continued his harrying tactics with renewed vigour as the great sailing galleons endeavoured to get under way. His galleys swept in as fast as the slaves could be beaten into driving them. In such conditions the huge, lumbering galleons made little headway. Stragglers were picked off and crushed. Barbarossa steadily gained the advantage. Unable to make full use of the now

favourable winds, Doria was faced with mounting losses as Barbarossa's galleys crashed and smashed into the sides of the great galleons and violent hand-to-hand fighting broke out with the Turks swarming aboard the Spanish vessels. Oars crashed into the sides of the ships, as smoke and flame filled the air. The hornets were stinging hard and true.

Andrea Doria saw that Barbarossa's fleet had almost surrounded the Spanish fleet – but he could do nothing about it. The superior tactics of the Turkish 'pirate' were gaining the upper hand and the huge galleons were falling to the smaller galleys.

Victory and defeat

Sunset brought respite as Barbarossa ordered his fleet to withdraw. He had lost many men and he knew he could not continue these harrying tactics much longer – the price of victory was mounting. But the prizes had been high also for he had accounted for five Spanish galleons. In the true pirate tradition of their Admiral, the Turkish ships were either sunk in action or destroyed by their crews – none had suffered the humiliation of capture.

That night Barbarossa slowly gathered his forces together, and with the captured galleons, waited for the dawn. The hours of darkness saw hasty repairs to the damaged galleys. Andrea Doria during the night, had decided to withdraw completely and as dawn broke his fleet was seen fast disappearing over the horizon, scurrying homewards. Barbarossa found himself without an enemy.

The Turks had won what became known as the Battle of Preveza, a holy battle. The 'pirate' Admiral, outnumbered and with smaller ships, had won the day. Here on September 28, 1537, Khair-ed-Din Barbarossa earned the title 'The King of the Seas'. On his return to Constantinople with his spoils he was feted and praised as only the victor of a mighty battle can be. His complete mastery and dominance of the Spanish and their allies, his ruggedness and ruthlessness in waiting for the right time and the ferocity with which he delivered his attacks made him a legend. Turkish-Moslem influence could now spread unchallenged through the Mediterranean. Thanks to Barbarossa a glorious future appeared assured for the Ottoman Empire.

Doria's fate was that of the vanquished servant of demanding masters. He had lost, he had run away when he should have fought to the death – so ran the thinking of the Papal dignitories, cosily removed from the cannon blasts and crashing timbers of the bloody conflict – and so he was charged with cowardice.

Above Victory at Preveza opened the way for the Turkish reconquest of Algeria and Tunis and established Moslem control of the Eastern Mediterranean.

Right Barbarossa lured Doria to the Gulf of Arta and then allowed himself to be 'tempted' out for a final battle on the open seas.

Preveza

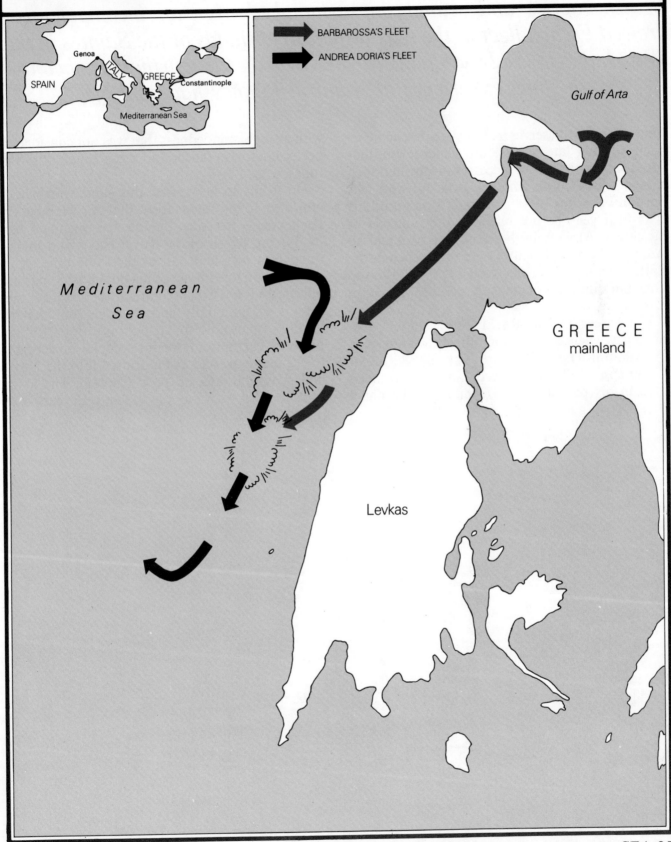

BARBAROSSA'S FLEET

ANDREA DORIA'S FLEET

Genoa

ITALY

SPAIN

GREECE

Constantinople

Mediterranean Sea

Gulf of Arta

Mediterranean Sea

G R E E C E
mainland

Levkas

THE SAINTS

British tactics and seamanship triumphed over an incompetently-crewed French fleet in the seas around the islands of the Saintes in the West Indies in 1782 and left the Royal Navy free to roam the Caribbean — the long experience of Admiral Rodney had paid off.

Fate sometimes reserves a man's greatest achievement for his later years, an achievement that surpasses all the other successes of his life. Such a man was George Brydges Rodney, who was born in February, 1718, and had to wait until his sixty-fifth year before reaching the pinnacle of his career. Already both a Knight Baron and an Admiral, his naval victory over the French in the Battle of the Saints, on April 12, 1782, allowed him the final accolade: an assured place in history.

His career in the Royal Navy started auspiciously when, as a young officer, he took part in Admiral Hawke's victory at the Battle of Ushant in 1747. He showed himself a ruthless man in his pursuit of 'prize money', chasing it with a single-mindedness that was not considered becoming for an officer and a gentleman of those times.

He seems to have used this same roughshod approach to his other career, that of a Member of Parliament. He was the elected member for Penryn, an officer of the Royal Navy, and something of a merchant, all at the same time. It is said he took advantage of his dual position as an officer and a Parliamentarian to advance the careers of his family and friends – but that is hardly remarkable in an age notorious for its political corruption. Against official objections, for example, he had a son drafted into the Navy and given the rank of 'post' Captain. The main objection was that the son was only 15 years old!

At the peak of the Battle of the Saints, with the 90-gun HMS Barfleur *firing into the French flagship, the 104-gun* Ville de Paris, *more than 60 men-of-war were engaged. French mistakes, and a change in the wind, allowed the British to bring them to battle although the French commander had planned only to exchange shots as he sailed by to escape into the Caribbean.*

Overleaf *The vigour of the British action, and their unorthodox tactics, scattered the French Fleet and as a result the British were able to sink many ships and capture others, including the* Ville de Paris.

Rodney sails

During his years as an active naval officer, he had fought against the greatest sea-powers of the day – the Spanish, the Dutch and the French. His year of destiny, 1782, saw him sailing from England towards the West Indies, where the French had been quietly assembling a fleet. With this fleet the French hoped to capture the main island of the West Indies, Jamaica. The French Fleet was commanded by Admiral Francois-Joseph-Paul Comte de Grasse, who, ironically, was attempting to set the seal on his own career.

Rodney had been sent to deal with this threat and had sailed from Plymouth on January 9, 1782. In just over a month his small fleet of 12 Royal Navy men-of-war were anchored in the harbour of the island of Barbados. The news that greeted him there was grim, for de Grasse was attacking the island of St. Kitts in his push northwards. The small British garrison on land and sea was holding out against tremendous odds. Supplies and ammunition were running out, and there was widespread disease amongst soldiers and sailors alike. It could only be a matter of time before de Grasse overwhelmed the island and continued his advance towards Jamaica.

A French success

Spending less than 48 hours in replenishing his stores from several merchant ships that happened to be in the port, Rodney sailed towards the beleaguered island. But it was too late – St. Kitts had fallen. Though the small naval force had managed to escape, de Grasse had finally succeeded in capturing the island. Rodney now joined the small escaping force and turned back to Barbados. Nothing could be done, so plans and tactics had to be reviewed.

Meanwhile, de Grasse swept on. The islands of Nevis and Monsarrat fell to him in quick succession. The French fleet was making tremendous inroads into the British-controlled territories. If the island of Jamaica fell to the French it would only be a matter of time before the Royal Navy was driven from the seas of the West Indies and the French would then have the rich undisputed mastery of Caribbean waters.

After the island of Monsarrat fell, Admiral de Grasse brought his fleet of 30 warships into Fort Royal, on the island of Martinique. There he planned his tactics for capturing the prize islands of Barbados and Antigua. His ships were replenished with stores and ammunition, and his hard-worked crews rested for the battle to come.

Sir George Brydges Rodney, who was now faced with the prospect of having to maintain a foothold for the British Empire in these waters, was also planning his strategy for a confrontation with de Grasse. He knew that de Grasse, lying at ease in the placid waters of Fort Royal, was planning his next move towards the final capture of his goal, Jamaica.

Waiting for a wind

Both men were impatient to start, but during those early spring weeks the weather was continually unsuitable. The ships of the line relied solely upon sail power, and therefore could not put to sea unless the winds were favourable.

Opposite Admiral George Brydges Rodney (1718-92), in a career that spanned the second half of the eighteenth century, fought the Spanish, the Dutch and the French, the major sea-powers of the day. His long experience gave him the advantage at the decisive Battle of the Saints.

Above Until this battle, Admiral Francois-Joseph-Paul, Comte de Grasse (1722-88) had had an equally distinguished career – but it ended with defeat.

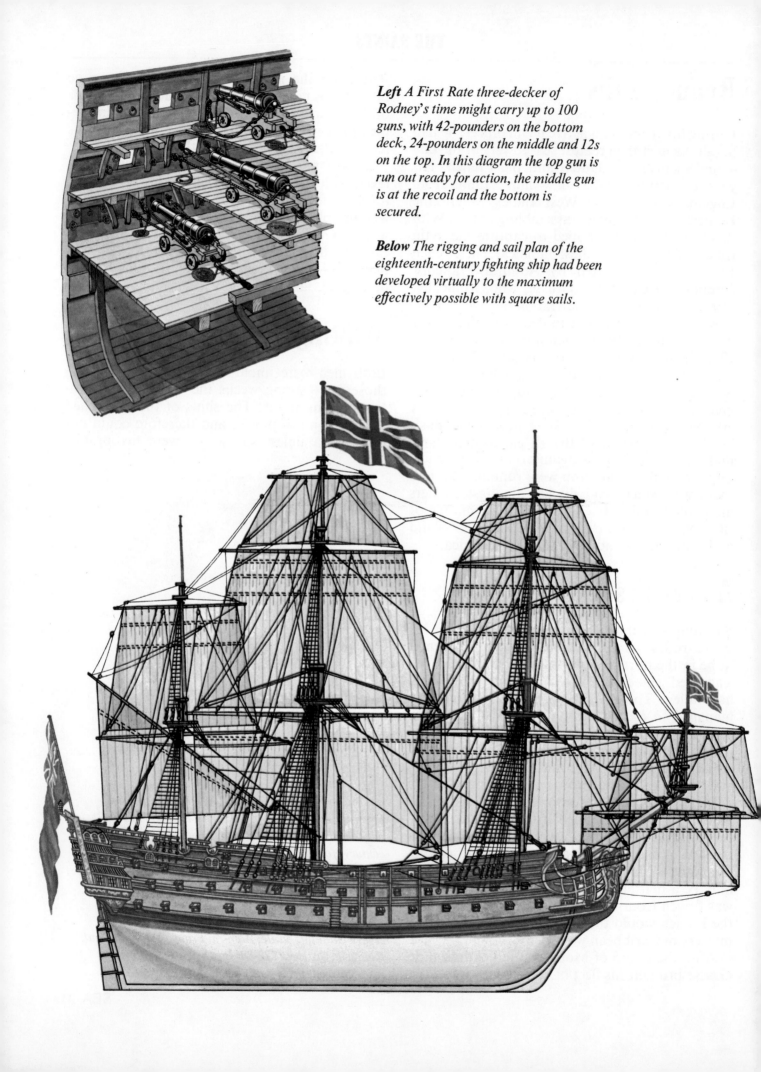

Left *A First Rate three-decker of Rodney's time might carry up to 100 guns, with 42-pounders on the bottom deck, 24-pounders on the middle and 12s on the top. In this diagram the top gun is run out ready for action, the middle gun is at the recoil and the bottom is secured.*

Below *The rigging and sail plan of the eighteenth-century fighting ship had been developed virtually to the maximum effectively possible with square sails.*

Week after week slipped by while the fleets anxiously waited for a break in the weather. Sometimes the winds were too light and sometimes too strong. With the light winds came heavy sea mists, and it was treacherous to put to sea in such conditions. If the winds were strong, manoeuvring the huge men-of-war became extremely difficult in the restricted passage-ways and channels.

So de Grasse and Rodney had no choice but to wait. They knew the weather would break with the coming of the late spring, and that suitable conditions would arrive. During these weeks of waiting, Rodney wrote home the following words: 'I'm of the opinion that the great events which must decide the Empire of the Ocean will be either off Jamaica or San Domingo.' Of this he was certain, his sense of strategy, and his years of experience telling him so. And, after all, he was a British Admiral, and would never be proved wrong. His vain nature told him that what he calculated would turn out to be true.

As the long wait drew on, news reached Rodney that must have jolted his confidence. French reinforcements had somehow slipped through his guard and had joined up with de Grasse. With these reinforcements of six men-of-war, and the 5,000 troops they were carrying, de Grasse now had a total of 36 ships. This was adequate for his rush northwards and the final phase of his operation, the capture of Jamaica itself.

Sir George Rodney had under his command 37 men-of-war. Some of them were from the force that had been stationed at St Kitts, some were from the West Indies' squadrons that had hastily been assembled, and some he had brought with him from England. It was a collection of warships of varying ages and varying degrees of reliability; men who had seen action rubbed shoulders with men who had never been in foreign waters before. But the weeks of waiting gave Sir George the opportunity to mould his forces and his age and experience enabled him to weld together the variety of ships and men into a fighting force.

The French fleet sails

The early summer of 1782 came to the Leeward Islands, bringing with it serene and fair weather. The winds moderated, and the sun shone brilliantly upon the clear blue waters. All was set for the battle. De Grasse gathered his fleet together and set sail. But they had been seen, for Rodney had positioned scouting frigates at strategic places in the channels and passages around Fort Royal. These ships had lain silently to watch for any French movements. On the night of April 6, the cruiser *Endymion* observed French activity within the port. The expected was happening, and the *Endymion* duly reported back to Rodney. As the *Endymion* scurried back with her news, the French fleet slid out of the port on a northerly course.

On hearing the news, Rodney immediately ordered his fleet to set sail in pursuit. The greater standard of discipline and seamanship that Rodney maintained now began to pay dividends. The great sailing warships, in perfect formation, slowly but surely made their way towards the French fleet – slowly, because the winds were now moderating and dropping. Offshore breezes, running from island to island, called for navigation and seamanship of the highest order so as to make the most profitable use of the light and airy conditions. Rodney had trained his crews well.

The strain begins to tell

Rodney's fleet closed with that of de Grasse. At times the two fleets could see one another in the perfect visibility, but yet little onward progress could be made. For several days, almost in slow motion, the fleets sailed on. The French were still heading northwards, with the British trying to overtake and stop them. In these extreme conditions frustration inevitably began to show itself in the French. Due to complete incompetence, the French warship *Zélé*, of 74-guns, collided with the 64-gun *Jason*.

Each ship had been endeavouring to catch the wind, and bad seamanship on the part of Lt. Gras-Préville, the Captain of the *Zélé*, brought about the collision. The *Jason* was so badly damaged that she hauled out of line and had to slowly make her way to Guadeloupe for repairs. De Grasse had lost a ship and not a shot had been fired yet. The *Zélé* had also been damaged, and on the morning of April 11, the 74-gunner was seen to be making very little headway, and was gradually slipping behind the rest of the French fleet. Rodney waited as the *Zélé* slowly came within his grasp.

Hour after hour in the airy conditions the ships

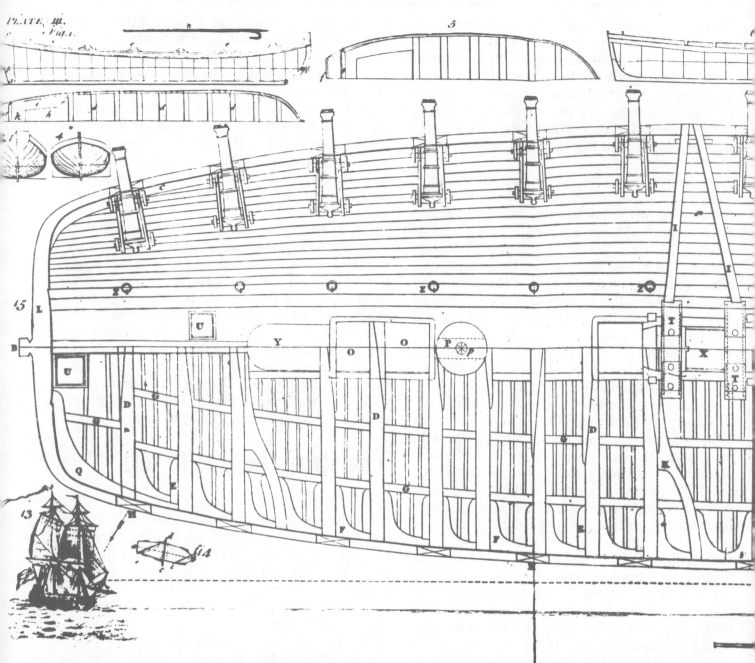

slipped towards one another. Hardly any winds filled their sails. For all the efforts of the crew of the *Zélé*, the distance between them and the on-coming British was steadily diminishing. Every yard of their canvas was aloft, but still she could not escape. Throughout that day the *Zélé*, at the very rear of the French fleet, strove to avoid the oncoming British. Night came and, with it, respite. The following morning the *Zélé* was no-where to be found – rather than allow inevitable slaughter she had been abandoned.

Still the main fleets were within sight of one another, but were well outside artillery range. Then, in his anxiety to push forward de Grasse made a fatal error. The scarcity of wind left him

with two possible decisions, for behind him Rod-ney's fleet was slowly bearing down upon him. De Grasse's alternatives were either to turn to leeward, which would bring him face to face with the British fleet, or to turn southwards and try to run the gauntlet. Working up as much speed as possible, de Grasse started on the latter course.

Line ahead

Rodney knew what to expect of the French. On seeing de Grasse fly his signals he ordered, at first light, his ships into the classic battle station of ships of the Royal Navy: 'line ahead', was the

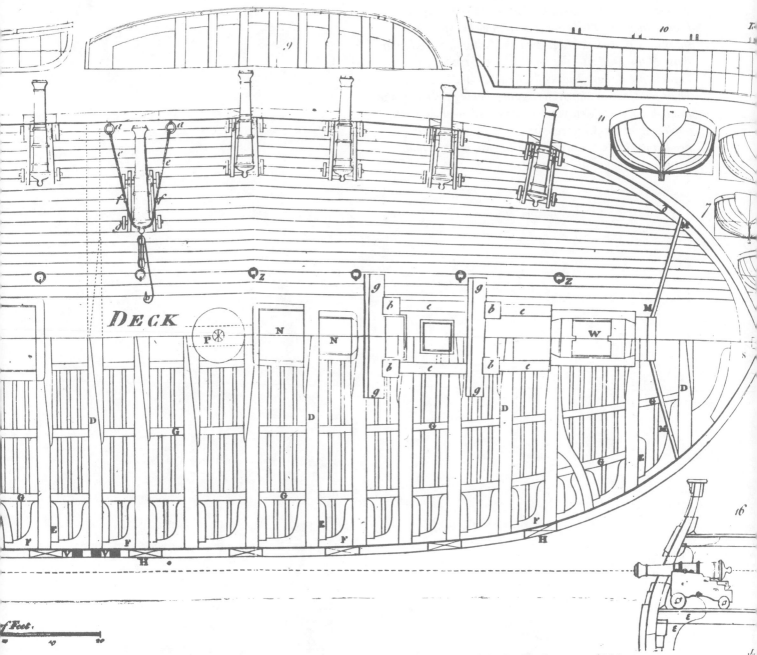

order – line ahead at two cables (1,200 feet) distance. The sails strained to catch every breath of the light wind, as the mighty men-of-war approached the French. De Grasse watched the British manoeuvring into formation, and ordered his own fleet into battle stations. This was also the classic 'line ahead' – but poor seamanship left the line stretched, with several gaps in it. The French ships moved towards the confrontation with the British, and steadily the two lines advanced head-on.

From first light the respective manoeuvres had taken less than three hours. Captain Taylor Penny, leading the British line in the *Marlborough*, opened fire at a range of 400 yards at the leading

A First Rate ship of the line had a crew of 850 men: servicing the heavy guns in battle, and there could be up to 30 42-pounders on the 180-foot main gun-deck, made exhaustive demands on manpower. The guns were muzzle loaders and after each shot had to be cleaned out, a charge of gunpowder up to half the weight of the shot put in, a wad of rope-yarn rammed home and the cannon ball or grape shot loaded. After priming the touch-hole with powder the gun was run up and fired either individually or as part of a broadside. And under fire all this took place with cannon balls shattering the ship's timbers, splinters flying amidst the smoke and noise so loud that many gunners were deafened.

THE SAINTS

Although outnumbered at the Battle of the Saints, the French theoretically held the advantage because their ships were more heavily gunned and better designed than those of the English – the English indeed tended to copy French ship design. Tactically, however, the French erred. Their tendency to aim at the rigging, hoping to cripple the English ships while staying at long range, would do little good in light airs when repairs were easy: the English fired at the hulls – between wind and water – and their better-served guns did far more damage.

French warship, the 74-gun *Hercule*. One by one the ships behind opened fire at their counterparts. The British *Arrogant*, the second in line, opened fire on the 74-gun *Neptune*, and the *Alcide*, of 74-guns, fired into the *Souverain*. Each ship attacked its opposite number as the lines passed each other.

Admiral Rodney opens fire

Rodney's own flagship, the mighty 90-gun *Formidable*, opened fire at a little after 8 a.m. It was actually impossible for Rodney to witness the whole scene, for with his ships in perfect line he was unable to see more than two or three ships either in front or behind. He was therefore un-

able to see precisely how the battle was faring at the head or stern of the great line.

Salvos ripped into the ships, as the distance between them was reduced to less than 100 feet. Shattered masts came tumbling down, to fall in disarray on the decks of the warships. Sails were torn from their shrouds, and the noise was deafening. Signals from ship to ship could not be made by loud-hailer, so they had to be made by hand. The massive barrage of the cannon ploughed into the French, and the French replied in kind. Smoke completely enveloped the ships. Records have it that Captain Savage, of the 74-gun *Hercules*, who had been wounded earlier on in the action, directed the operations of his ship from a chair. Unable to be heard above the tremendous noise, he was seen signalling frantically at the gunners to fire between wind and water to sink the French rascals.

An hour of this terrible exchange took place, an hour in which the lines came exactly head to tail. At this point Rodney's pre-arranged tactics came into play. Catching as much of the light winds as possible, the centre of the British line turned inwards by a pre-arranged order to break the straggling French line. The French ships were forced to bear away. Immediately a large gap opened up in the French line, and Rodney in the *Formidable* started the rout.

The rout begins

The French man-of-war *Glorieux* was singled out and came in for heavy punishment as the *Formidable* bore down upon her and at point-blank range fired withering broadsides into her. So close did the ships pass that their spars became entangled for a second. The *Formidable* was pouring tremendous punishment into the side of the French man-of-war, and when she had passed the next in line, the 90-gun *Namur*, continued the uneven struggle. The *Namur* blasted round after round into the *Glorieux'* weeping side. The *Glorieux* ceased fire with smoke pouring from her gun ports, her masts askew, and her

De Grasse's flagship, the Ville de Paris *was the largest and most heavily-armed ship in the two fleets, and in de Grasse's eyes the key to the Caribbean. When he hauled down his colours, after ten hours of fighting, French power in the West Indies had been broken.*

sails torn to shreds. Slowly through the gaping wounds in her sides came the sound of cracking and crashing as her bulkheads gave way. Water poured into her and she settled into the water up to her ports.

The *Formidable* was still leading the attack: with five other men-of-war, she was ploughing into the disorganized French. The enemy was being scattered, and in the scattering became easy prey. But a lull now settled upon the battle. Every square yard of canvas was hoisted aloft, for the fickle winds had dropped, making manoeuvring impossible. It was as if the entire battle had been frozen. Ships could hardly make way, but there was at least the compensation that very quick repairs could be made. Sails that had been torn were hurriedly replaced, and the wounded were given hurried treatment.

After less than an hour, the sails began to fill as a light breeze returned. The ships once more commenced battle, and the French were by now in complete disarray. From the *Formidable* Rodney, together with his other ships, harried the disordered French. Ship after ship was attacked individually and laid bare, its masts brought down and its hulls rendered smoking pyres. Past noon and well into the afternoon the rout continued. As the battle progressed British colours were hoisted in the much-damaged *Glorieux;* the *Cesar* was captured, and later the *Hector* capitulated. De Grasse was indeed suffering a terrible defeat. His plan of French domination of the Caribbean, based on the capture of Jamaica, was being blasted to shreds before his eyes.

Rodney reaps his reward

At just after 6.30 p.m. de Grasse ordered his colours to be struck from the mast of his flagship, the *Ville de Paris*. Rodney then ordered the action to be broken off: the French had surrendered. That night the British fleet surrounded the French ships that had capitulated, and in the morning de Grasse came on board the *Formidable*, to remain there for two days as the 'guest' of Admiral Rodney. The British escorted, or towed, the captured vessels of the French fleet into Port Royal harbour, Jamaica. There they anchored on April 29.

The aging Admiral Rodney had gained a victory that had ensured the Royal Navy's domination of the seas of the Caribbean. Any threat of a

French invasion had been completely averted. Rodney himself had gained many prize ships, and was later to write of his career: 'Within two little years I have taken two Spanish, one Dutch, and one French Admiral.'

De Grasse, on being returned to his homeland, was virtually ordered to retire from the Navy. A sad man, he died in 1788, some six years after his defeat at the hands of Rodney. Ten years after the Battle of The Saints, Admiral Rodney died, safe in the knowledge that he had written his name for ever in the annals of the history of the sea. By supreme single-mindedness he had brought a rich conclusion to his life and saved the vast wealth of the West Indies for the British Empire.

Ships in the Battle of the Saints

BRITISH FLEET

Name	Guns	Name	Guns
Formidable (Flagship)	90	Marlborough	74
Agamemnon	64	Monarch	74
Ajax	74	Montagu	74
Alcide	74	Namur	90
Alfred	74	Nonsuch	64
America	64	Prince George	90
Anson	64	Prince William	64
Arrogant	74	Princessa	70
Barfleur	90	Prothee	64
Bedford	74	Repulse	64
Belliqueux	64	Resolution	74
Canada	74	Royal Oak	74
Centaur	74	Russell	74
Conqueror	74	St Albans	64
Duke	90	Torbay	74
Fame	74	Valiant	74
Hercules	74	Warrior	74
Magnificent	74	Yarmouth	64

FRENCH FLEET

Name	Guns	Name	Guns
Ville de Paris (Flagship)*	104	Hector*	74
Ardent*	64	Hercule	74
Auguste	80	Languedoc	80
Bourgogne	74	Magnanime	74
Brave	74	Magnifique	74
César*	74	Marseillais	74
Citoyen	74	Neptune	74
Conquerant	74	Northumberland	74
Couronne	80	Palmier	74
Dauphin Royal	70	Pluton	74
Destin	74	Réfléchi	74
Diadéme	74	Sceptre	74
Duc de Bourgogne	80	Scipion	74
Eveillé	64	Souverain	74
Glorieux*	74	Triomphant	80

Vessels captured.

Tactics decided the Battle of the Saints – so called because it took place in the Passage of the Saintes to the north of the island of Dominica. The two fleets were set to pass each other in line ahead when Rodney managed to turn the British ships in three sections into gaps in the French line – the first commander to use the technique. The French never recovered from their surprise at having to fight at close quarters and ultimately surrendered.

The Saints

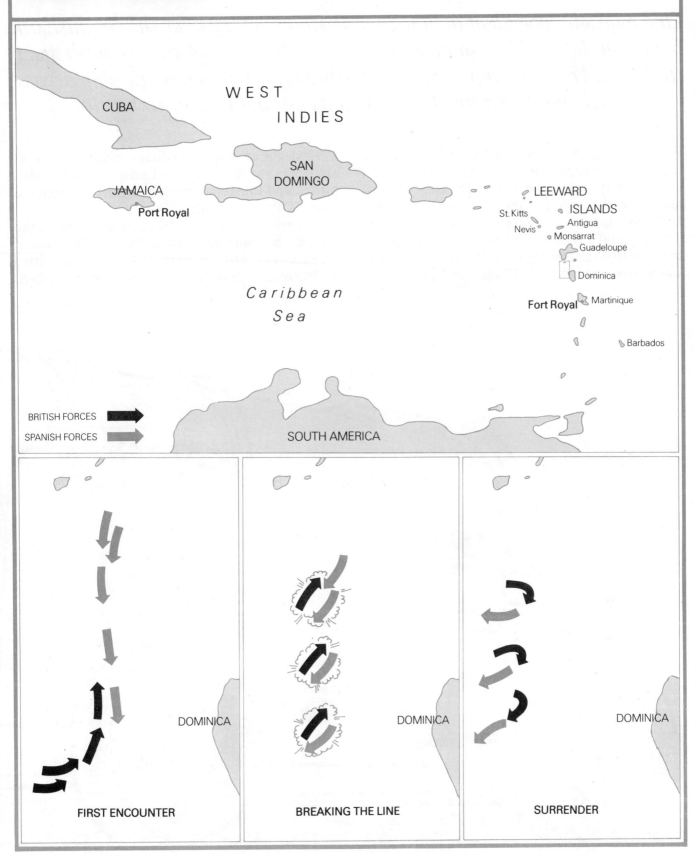

WEST

INDIES

CUBA

JAMAICA

Port Royal

SAN
DOMINGO

LEEWARD

ISLANDS

St. Kitts

Nevis

Antigua

Monsarrat

Guadeloupe

Dominica

Fort Royal

Martinique

Caribbean

Sea

Barbados

BRITISH FORCES

SPANISH FORCES

SOUTH AMERICA

DOMINICA

DOMINICA

DOMINICA

FIRST ENCOUNTER

BREAKING THE LINE

SURRENDER

CAPE ST VINCENT

One man's independent action gave Britain victory over the Spanish off Cadiz in 1797. That man was Horatio Nelson: as the Spanish fleet turned and ran virtually without fighting he swung his single ship across their path and by sheer audacity brought them to battle.

An embattled nation, Britain by 1797 was reeling under the hammer blows of France's greatest soldier, Napoleon Bonaparte. Disaster on disaster rained down as French troops swept into Italy, robbing Britain of its naval bases of Naples, Tuscany and Leghorn. The proud sea nation was being driven relentlessly from the Mediterranean. Then Spain allied with France and in October 1797 declared war on Britain who now stood alone against the might of Europe, isolated, dispirited and threatened with being driven from the shore of the continent.

The grim spectre of defeat stared Britain in the face. If she could not control the seas her natural defences counted for nothing. Napoleon's drive to European domination could not be halted.

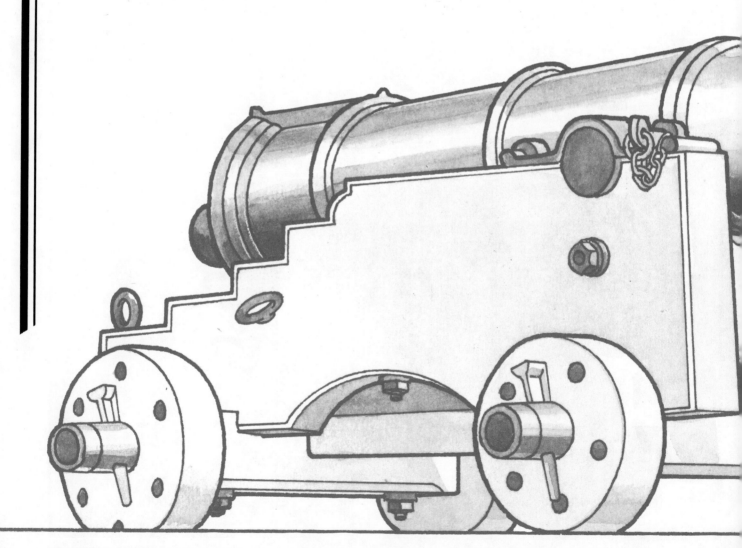

Then, with the last gasp of morale ebbing away, the man of the moment stepped forward to save the nation. That man was Horatio Nelson.

Born in 1758, in the tiny village of Burnham Thorpe in Norfolk, Horatio Nelson was the sixth child of the Reverend Edmund Nelson and his wife Catherine. Brought up in the strict atmosphere of a Christian household, the young Horatio was encouraged to fend for himself. In doing so he acquired his fascination with the sea. He spent hours watching the grey, foam-flecked waters of the stormy North Sea, seeing a whole spectrum of ships sail by. There were lumbering cargo ships, plying their trade along Britain's East coast, squadrons of warships, each magnificently bedecked and sailing by in perfect formation and ships of the line, mighty Royal ships.

There was no more romantic introduction to the prospect of a career on the high seas.

A Captain at 21

In 1770, at the tender age of 12 years, Horatio entered the service of the Royal Navy, as a midshipman on a Third Rate ship of the line, the 1,386 ton *Raisonnable*. In these early years Nelson learnt discipline above all else – discipline in handling a ship of the line and discipline in leading men. He spent many years learning the arts of true navigation, seamanship and the tactics of seaborne warfare.

Nelson progressed rapidly: in 1777 he became Second Lieutenant in the 32-gun *Lowestoffe*;

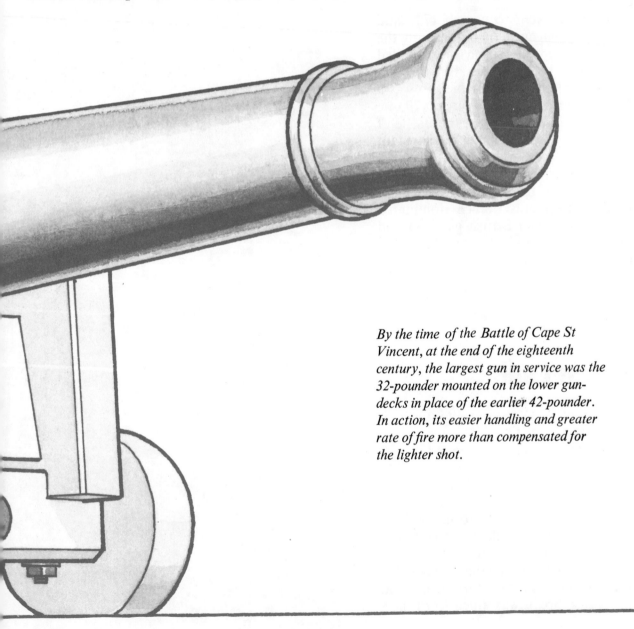

By the time of the Battle of Cape St Vincent, at the end of the eighteenth century, the largest gun in service was the 32-pounder mounted on the lower gun-decks in place of the earlier 42-pounder. In action, its easier handling and greater rate of fire more than compensated for the lighter shot.

Inset left Horatio Nelson (1758-1805) displayed the initiative that made him one of the greatest naval commanders of all time in turning his ship across the Spanish line. His action allowed **inset right** Admiral John Jervis, who had already smashed his way through the Spanish line, to bring the Spaniards to battle and defeat them. In the hotly-fought action the British captured four ships and seriously damaged ten more without a single loss.

1778 saw him commander of the 138-ton brig *Badger*; and within six months he was in command of the 557-ton 28-gun frigate *Hinchinbrook*. Horatio Nelson had hoisted his Captain's pennant before he was 21 years old. In the following years, Nelson served in North America, Jamaica, Nicaragua, South America and the West Indies.

Britain and France went to war in 1793 and Nelson was shortly engaged in battle with the French fleet. In 1794, on July 12, he was wounded and lost the sight of his right eye. But this setback did not mar his progress, for Nelson was a singleminded servant of his country. In 1795 he fought at the Gulf of Genoa and at the Battle of Hyéres. The French were becoming his constant enemy.

In 1797 Nelson was despatched on a hazardous mission in command of the frigate *Minerve*. His aim was to raid deep into French dominated waters and bring the small British garrison and naval stores from the island of Elba. The *Minerve* ran into two Spanish frigates but Nelson's brilliant seamanship outsmarted the Spanish men-of-war and he fulfilled his task completely.

He then returned to join the English fleet under its Admiral, Sir John Jervis.

Two fleets at Cadiz

Jervis had been sent to keep continuous watch off the Spanish coast, near Cadiz, for any movements of the Spanish fleet commanded by its admiral, Don José de Cordoba. The mighty Spanish fleet of two divisions, totalling 27 ships, had been stationed for some time at Cadiz. Jervis was waiting for the Spanish fleet to move from the harbour so that battle could be joined and, he hoped, Spain's naval fighting force destroyed. This would effectively drive the wedge for Britain's re-entry into the Mediterranean, and would also, because Spain was allied to France,

CAPE ST VINCENT

The 100-gun Victory, *flagship of the fleet commander at Cape St Vincent, Sir John Jervis, and largest ship in the British fleet, was herself overshadowed by the massive 130-gun Spanish flagship* Santisima Trinidad.

strike a blow directly against Bonaparte.

Jervis's small fleet numbered only 15 ships of the line. Six of these, including his flagship the *Victory*, had 100 guns, and a further eight had 74 guns each. The 1639-ton *Captain*, Horatio Nelson's ship, was one of these.

The flagship of Admiral Don José de Cordoba was an enormous 130-gun four-decked ship, the *Santisima Trinidad*. As well as this mighty flagship de Cordoba had six warships each carrying 112 guns, two carrying 80 guns and 18 other vessels carrying at least 74 guns. His was a mighty armada, a great fighting, battling force, but Admiral Jervis was not daunted. Although he

had only 15 ships, his men had been schooled in the highest standards of Royal Navy training.

The Spanish fleet, Jervis knew, was frail despite its appearance. The massive Spanish ships were under-crewed and the officers were poorly trained. Further, the guns were manned by soldiers, not seamen, for the seamen had not been instructed in the art of seaborne warfare! Anticipation riffled through the small English fleet stationed off Cadiz as it prepared for the coming battle with de Cordoba's armada.

The Spanish fleet was sighted on February 14, 1797 at 8.15 a.m. In perfect morning visibility, they were seen sailing in two divisions, line ahead. Admiral Jervis ordered his ships into close order, single line ahead. HMS *Captain*, Nelson's ship was placed three from the rear. The English plan was to steer between the two groups of Spanish men-o-war and then turn to destroy the large group with concentrated fire power. The English ships were no match in sheer size for the mighty Spanish warships – but Jervis accepted the risk.

The chase is on

Jervis's foresight and superior naval skill soon became apparent. The Spanish, on seeing the British Navy advance, failed to close their ranks; the Spanish seamen, so inexperienced, could not maintain good close order. Their ships started to straggle out into two vague groups and Jervis at once seized the initiative. The English bore down upon the disordered Spanish fleet like a hungry wolf pack. The Spanish panicked and tried vainly to regroup into one main defensive body. The English were in pursuit.

Belatedly the leading Spanish ships altered course to port in an attempt to fall back to their main body. Jervis responded with the dramatic signal to his ships. 'Pass through the enemy's line.' The bold approach gained the success it deserved because the Spanish could not close their ranks in time. Led by Captain Thomas Troubridge, in the 74-gun *Culloden*, the perfect line of British warships bore into the weak belly of the Spanish fleet. The British opened fire and a fusilade of shots ripped into the Spanish ships. The huge, three-decked flagship of the Spanish Vice Admiral, the 112-gun *Principe de Asturias*, was heavily raked. Her topmasts were shattered, her sails blown to shreds, her masts splintered

under the enormous fire power and flames started to lick her decks.

De Cordoba ordered the confused Spanish fleet to alter course to north in an attempt to shake off his pursuers. Jervis countered by tacking his ships about in succession. The enemy was now being raked with withering broadsides as cannon upon cannon was brought to bear on the lumbering Spanish warships.

Nelson makes his move

The battle, which had been a series of engagements between passing ships, reached its peak at 1 p.m. One after another, Admiral Jervis's warships had poured fire into the Spanish fleet, and had escaped virtually unscathed. But then an opportunity presented itself – the Spanish found themselves in a position where they could run for safety. Yet as they tried to flee from the clutches of the wolves, Horatio Nelson entered the scene.

Nelson had watched the battle from HMS *Captain* and his brilliant independent spirit now came into play. He quickly sized up the situation. Ignoring Jervis's orders of maintaining line and battle stations, Nelson took the *Captain* out to port, swinging away from the rear of the British fleet. He then reversed course through 180 degrees. This manoeuvre brought him face to face with the escaping enemy. The *Captain* then headed into the main Spanish body.

Ploughing forward with all the speed he could muster, Nelson produced a single-handed thrust into de Cordoba's fleet. The Spanish were amazed to see such audacity from a 74-gun ship: a small Third Rate vessel was challenging the massive 130-gun ships of the Spanish fleet. The *Captain* bore down upon the Spanish ships and once in range Nelson gave the order: 'Open fire!' The *Captain's* guns blazed at the enemy ships on the fringe of the main body. The Spanish were taken aback – and the immediate advantage fell to Nelson.

Seeing the *Captain* pull out of line, Captain Cuthbert Collingwood, in the 74-gun *Excellent*, Captain Thomas Elfrederick, in the 90-gun *Blenheim*, and several others swung out of line and rushed into support. The rout was now on. Nelson in the *Captain*, had closed upon the flagship, the *Santisima Trinidad*, and a tremendous bombardment was exchanged.

CAPE ST VINCENT

'Raked her both ahead and stern' says the log of the
Victory **centre left** of one engagement during the battle.
Victory's guns sent 32-pound cannon balls into the sides of
the Spanish ships, shattering timbers and creating great
confusion on deck.

Broadside after broadside

Still the *Captain* bore on, pouring broadside after broadside into the bemused enemy. The *Blenheim* and the *Excellent*, passing to windward, joined in. Masts came crashing down, sails were torn apart and smoke billowed, cloaking the Spanish fleet. Onlookers could barely see the British ships wrestling with the Spanish men-of-war. So violent and so intense was the action that the Third Rate 74-gun *Culloden* was crippled and the *Blenheim* beaten back.

The badly mauled *Captain*, after hauling away from the *Santisima Trinidad*, found herself alongside the damaged 80-gun *San Nicholas*. Nelson, in a remarkable feat of navigation, brought the

battered *Captain* alongside the *San Nicholas*. At the head of a boarding party, Nelson swept on to the decks of the Spanish ship. A running hand-to-hand-fight developed. Sheer ferocity overwhelmed the Spanish in a brief, bloody battle. The Spanish ensign was hauled down and Nelson took possession of a prize Spanish man-of-war.

The *Excellent* engaged the *Salvador del Mundo*, then passed forward on to the *San Ysidro* which

Captain Collingwood engaged at close quarters. Driving alongside he boarded the Spaniard, and again, after a very quick and one-sided action the Spanish flag was hauled down.

The *Santisima Trinidad* after some tremendous punishment struck her flag from the mast – she was capitulating. Jervis was overjoyed and he signalled his fleet to come to windward. But while he was re-positioning his fleet, the *Santisima*

A cross-section of the Victory, *the British flagship at Cape St Vincent and Nelson's ship 8 years later at Trafalgar. Designed by Sir Thomas Slade,* Victory *was launched on May 7, 1765 and became one of the greatest fighting ships of her time.*

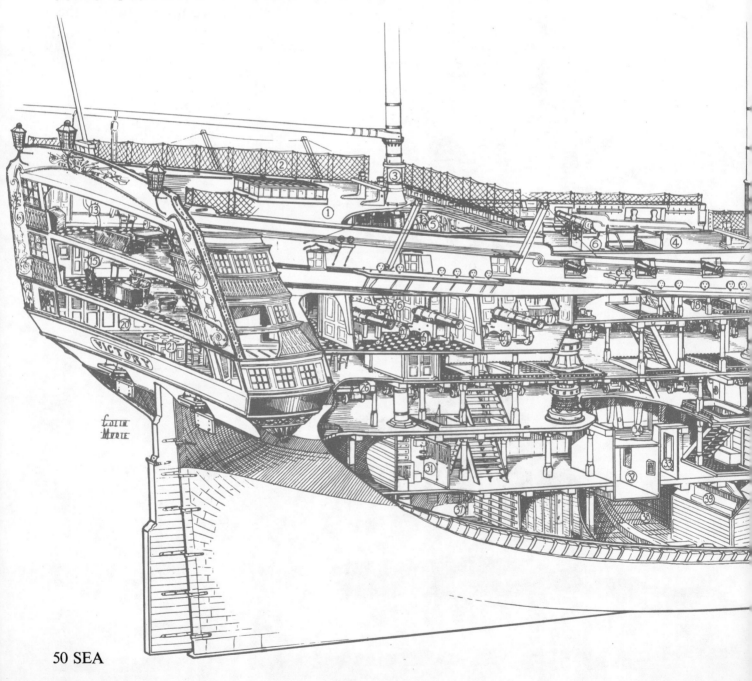

Key to diagram

1 *Poop*
2 *Hammock nettings*
3 *Mizzenmast*
4 *Quarterdeck*
5 *Steering wheels*
6 *(Nelson fell in 1805)*
7 *Pikes*
8 *Mainmast*
9 *Gangway*
10 *Foc's'le*
11 *Carronades*

12 *Foremast*
13 *Captain's cabin*
14 *Upper deck*
15 *Admiral's day-cabin*
16 *Admiral's dining-cabin*
17 *Admiral's sleeping-cabin*
18 *Shot garlands*
19 *Middle deck*
20 *Wardroom*
21 *Tiller head*
22 *Entry port*

23 *Capstan head*
24 *Galley and Stove*
25 *Lower deck*
26 *Tiller*
27 *Chain Pumps*
28 *Mooring bitts*
29 *Manger*
30 *Orlop*
31 *Sick-bay*
32 *Aft hanging magazine*
33 *Lamp room*

34 *(Nelson died in 1805)*
35 *Forward magazine*
36 *Powder store*
37 *Powder room*
38 *Aft hold*
39 *Shot locker*
40 *Well*
41 *Main hold*
42 *Cable store*
43 *Main magazine*
44 *Filling room*

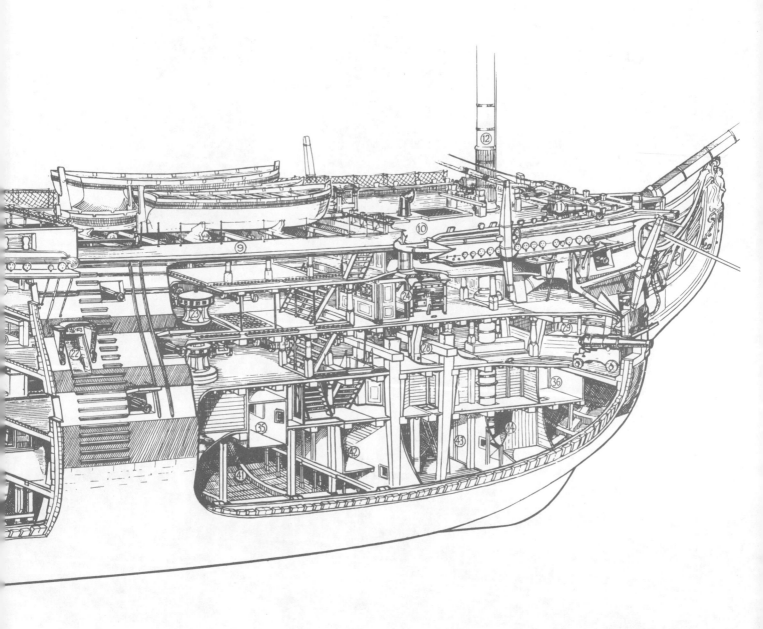

Above *Nelson's bold action in his ship the* Captain *brought him two personal prizes – the* San Josef *and the* San Nicholas, *both major Spanish ships. Here Nelson boards the* San Josef. *After a brief, bloody struggle the Spaniards surrendered.*

Below *Shredded sails and shattered timbers marked the ships that survived this hard-fought battle.*

Trinidad, taking a chance escaped. The largest war vessel then afloat escaped from the clutches of the Royal Navy; escaped to fight again eight years later at the Battle of Trafalgar.

A stunning victory

But Nelson's action, his fine initiative when all appeared to have been lost, enabled Admiral Jervis to claim four excellent prize vessels, the *San Josef*, the *Salvador del Mundo* (both of these ships were larger than most of the British First Rate ships), the *San Nicholas* and the *San Ysidro*. Admiral Jervis had not lost one ship and had suffered only 300 casualties.

Cape St Vincent was a stunning British victory. The Spanish had lost four ships, had suffered serious damage to ten more and their casualties were over 800. Jervis was pleased – but the prize, the *Santisima Trinidad*, had slipped through his fingers.

The following day the British shaped course for Lagos, while the remains of the Spanish fleet withdrew, under cover of night, to Cadiz.

When the news reached Britain of the tremendous victory, morale immediately rose; the joint threat of France and Spain together was dispelled. Britain's rulers richly rewarded their heroes. Jervis became an Earl and took the title Earl St Vincent from his victory. All the subordinate Admirals were made Baronets, and Nelson, promoted to the rank of Rear-Admiral, was created a Knight of the Bath. It was by his brilliant independent action and excellent judgement that victory had been won.

The gate to the Mediterranean had been reopened. Admiral Nelson's name now became a household word and from this time on his fellow countrymen were to heap honour upon honour on him. His decision on that St Valentine's Day in 1797, to turn the *Captain* out of line and prevent the Spanish fleet escaping, proved beyond doubt that the man of the moment had arrived. His action inspired the nation and the war against France and Spain was renewed with great vigour.

Nelson had cut his teeth in this violent battle, and proved he was a brilliant naval leader. He was to rise, in the years to come, to greater things, and greater honours. The culmination was the British naval victory of 1805 in the battle that was fought off Cape Trafalgar, when Horatio Nelson gave his life for his beloved country.

Ships in the Battle of Cape St Vincent

BRITISH FLEET

Name	Guns	Name	Guns
Victory	100	Diadem	64
(Flagship)		Egmont	74
Barfleur	98	Excellent	74
Blenheim	98	Goliath	74
Britannia	100	Irresistible	74
Captain	74	Namur	90
Colossus	74	Orion	74
Culloden	74	Prince George	98

SPANISH FLEET

Name	Guns	Name	Guns
Santisima Trinidad	130	Salvador del Mundo*	112
(Flagship)		San Antonio	74
Atlante	74	San Domingo	74
Bahama	74	San Formin	74
Concepcion	112	San Francisco de Paula	74
Conde de Regla	112	San Genaro	74
Conquistador	74	San Ildefonso	74
Firme	74	San Josef*	112
Glorioso	74	San Juan Nepomuceno	74
Mexicano	112	San Nicholas*	80
Neptuno	80	San Pablo	74
Oriente	74	San Ysidro*	74
Pèlayo	74	Soberano	74
Principe de Asturias	112	Terrible	74

Vessels captured

Right *The location of the battle of Cape St Vincent and the disposition of the opposing fleets came about because Admiral John Jervis saw the chance to cut off the Spanish fleet from its base at Cadiz and, by destroying it, open up the Mediterranean for the British.*

Cape St Vincent

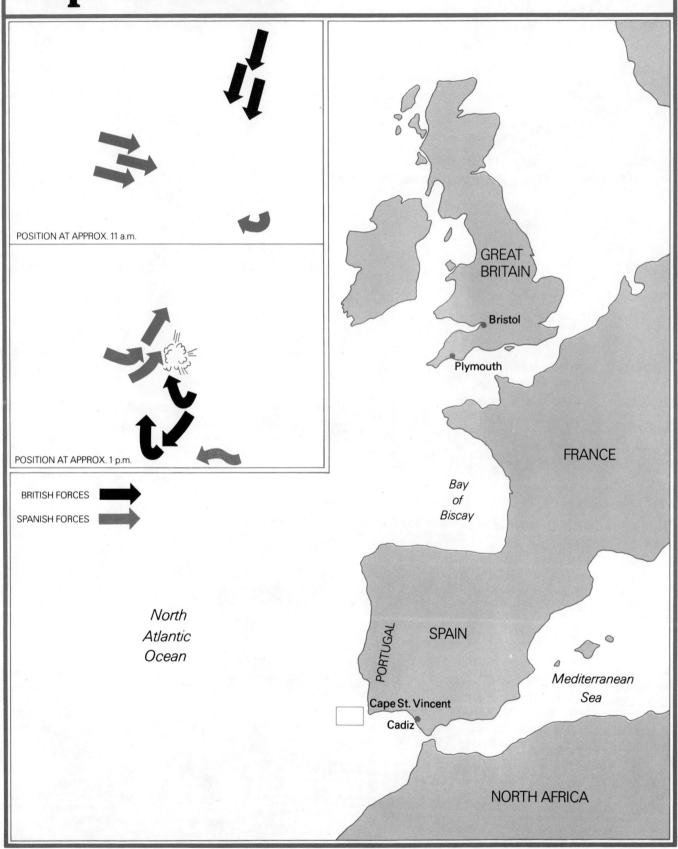

POSITION AT APPROX. 11 a.m.

POSITION AT APPROX. 1 p.m.

BRITISH FORCES

SPANISH FORCES

GREAT BRITAIN

Bristol

Plymouth

FRANCE

Bay of Biscay

North Atlantic Ocean

PORTUGAL

SPAIN

Cape St. Vincent

Cadiz

Mediterranean Sea

NORTH AFRICA

Stark example of crushing defeat – a wrecked Russian battleship lies at anchor in Port Arthur. The defeat of the Imperial Russian fleet at Tsushima was total.

TSUSHIMA STRAIT

Halfway round the world for a rendezvous with disaster — that was the fate of the Russian fleet in 1905. As the pride of Russia set out the aim was vengeance against the Japanese, but at Tsushima Strait Admiral Togo annihilated the Russians and broke their power.

During the nineteenth century the European powers established almost complete dominion over the lands of the East. By the last quarter of the century, China and India had been reduced to the status of mere provinces of various European empires. Only Japan had managed to preserve its national sovereignty, maintaining her natural insular isolation until she realized that, to survive in the East, it was apparently necessary to use western methods and ideas.

Japan therefore 'westernized' her army, navy, industry and large sections of her whole society, in the space of 25 years. But in doing all this, she inevitably started to compete with some of the European powers she sought to emulate. In 1904, diplomatic relations with Tsarist Russia were near to breaking point. Both countries had long considered war an inevitable conclusion to their rivalry and the war that did finally break out between them is known as the Russo-Japanese war. It represents a turning point in the history of the modern world, for it was the first time an eastern nation successfully engaged a European power.

East against West

In preparing for this war, the Russians had steadily built up their fleets in the Far East. At Port Arthur (modern Lu-shun) in Manchuria, they had grouped seven battleships, seven cruisers, 20 destroyers and many gun-boats and smaller vessels. All were of modern construction, with well-drilled crews and efficient officers. In the port of Vladivostok they had gathered together a smaller force, consisting of three large cruisers and one small cruiser, together with many torpedo-boats.

The Japanese wanted above all to capture Port Arthur and at least part of the massive flotilla that was based there. By dealing the Tsarist forces such a damaging blow they would win control of the sea lanes of the Far East. This, then, was their ultimate objective, and a rich prize it was. The master-mind behind the Japanese plan was the brilliant tactician and naval strategist Vice-Admiral Heihachiro Togo.

In the early part of 1904 their plans were finally ready to be put into action. On February 6 Vice-Admiral Togo told his officers: 'The Russian fleet is massed at Port Arthur, prepare to sail at once. Annihilate the enemy and set His Majesty's heart at ease!' Diplomatic relations with Tsarist Russia were cut the following afternoon, and on the night of February 8, Togo despatched ten torpedo-boats to attack the Russian ships at anchor in Port Arthur. Togo realized that his moves had to bring quick and decisive victory before Russia was able to bring up her massive reserves.

A Japanese success

In the approaches to Port Arthur lay the un-suspecting Russian battle fleet. The Japanese torpedo-boats approached stealthily under the cover of night, only to find that the Tsarists appeared to be making their task even simpler. The cruiser *Pallada* was making half-hearted attempts to patrol the entrance to the port, and in doing so, had all of her powerful searchlights switched on. This meant that the Japanese torpedo-boats could pick their targets almost at leisure. They steamed past the Russians in two groups of five, and each boat then discharged her torpedoes into the heart of the Russian ships. Having delivered their deadly weapons they turned away sharply at full speed.

In all, of the 18 torpedoes fired only three were effective – but effective these three certainly were. The cruiser *Pallada* was struck amidships and her coal bunkers set on fire. The First Class battleship *Retvizan* was hit on the port side, having a hole 220 feet square torn in her. Another battleship, the *Tsarvitch*, was struck in the aft magazine. This hit shattered her bulkheads and flooded the steering compartment.

The action was quickly over and had been a brilliant initial success for the Japanese. They themselves suffered neither hits nor casualties. The Russians had been foolishly complacent and they had paid the price. The Japanese, on the other hand, had struck just as Togo had intended, quickly and accurately.

On the morning after the attack, Togo brought up his heavy guns and, at long range, poured fire into the rest of the Tsarist fleet. Having thrown the Russians into confusion by the speed of his first thrust, he now pressed home his advantage. Within a few hours the Russian fleet had taken severe damage. The cost to Togo this time was only six Japanese lives. In the space of just 24 hours, the complete balance of naval power in the Far East had been reversed.

After this successful opening, Togo put the second stage of his plan into operation. Port Arthur was put under blockade by the Japanese fleet. Admiral Togo blockaded the naval base and was content to keep the crippled Russian ships bottled up. He knew that this effectively rendered the Russian ships powerless and he had only to wait until the Japanese troops encircled Port Arthur on the landward side for the port to be his for the taking.

The Russians fight back

Total victory, however, was not to come quite so easily, because now the Russians produced their most brilliant tactician and naval officer, Admiral Stephan Ossipovich Makarov and ordered him to command the remains of the beleaguered

fleet penned up in Port Arthur. His orders were simply to bring the remains of the fleet into top fighting condition and then to crush the Imperial forces. This was indeed a commission to tax all Makarov's skill as a commander, and he did not shrink from it.

Togo and Makarov were admirable adversaries: Togo attempting to strangle Makarov into submission and Makarov endeavouring to break Togo's grip. But fate was again on the side of the Imperial Japanese. After more than a month of continually harassing the Japanese blockaders, Makarov's flagship struck a Japanese mine while returning from a raid and blew up. Makarov was killed, and his loss was a terrible blow to the besieged Russians at Port Arthur. Despondency now set in amongst the Tsarist troops, as the scales tipped again in favour of Togo's forces.

All was not well with the Imperial Japanese Navy, however. The damage inflicted by Admiral Makarov in his daring raids, added to the enormous resources needed to keep up the blockade, were taking their toll. The drain on Togo's strength involved in applying a death grip to the Tsarist Navy was considerable. He realized that he had to bring about the complete destruction of Port Arthur quickly, or the Tsarist fish would get off his hook.

Half round the world

In St Petersburg (modern Leningrad), the news from Port Arthur had been received with consternation. A decision was quickly taken to send reinforcements to the Tsarist fleet. But this was where the heart of the Russians' problem lay, for they could only be sent from St Petersburg, and that was half-way around the world.

So it was on October 9, 1904, that Tsar Nicholas II despatched the reinforcements for Port Arthur from the naval base of Reval. The Tsar was sending the newly-completed battleship *Kniaz Suvarov* along with her sister-ships, the *Orel*, *Vorodino*, and *Imperator Alexander III*. These battleships were the backbone of a mighty fleet which the Russians regarded as invincible: Admiral Togo would surely be crushed by this force. The main problem was that of speed – the Russian reinforcements had to reach Port Arthur as quickly as possible. All the while, Togo had virtually a free hand to bring up his own reserves and make his own plans

for the inevitable battle that would decide the issue.

The vast Russian armada that set sail for the Far East consisted of 42 vessels, and the man chosen to command was one of the most senior officers in the Tsar's Navy, Vice-Admiral Zinovy Petrovich Rozhdestvensky. Rozhdestvensky, devoted to the Navy, to his Tsar and to his country, was a man of great intelligence who had reached the high rank of Vice Admiral strictly on his merits. A brilliant commander and tactician, he spared himself even less than he spared his men. He demanded the best of himself and his men, and he usually obtained both.

Soon after the fleet started on its 18,000 mile voyage to Port Arthur, an incident occurred that demonstrated to Rozhdestvensky just how great was the need to spend the voyage in training his inexperienced crews. On October 22, as the Russian fleet was passing through the southern reaches of the North Sea, the nervous and obviously frightened Russian gunners mistook a fleet of British trawlers for Japanese

Opposite In line ahead formation and with battle ensigns hoisted, Admiral Togo's fleet steams confidently towards the Russian adversary.

Above left Given command of the Russian Baltic fleet, Vice-Admiral Rozhdestvensky had the unenviable task of sailing 18,000 miles to the Pacific to do battle with the Japanese. The battle was lost and just three years later Rozhdestvensky died, a sad and embittered man.

Above right Admiral Heimachoro Togo was a ruthless and resourceful commander of the Imperial Japanese fleet.

destroyers! On seeing these trawlers in the half-light, they immediately opened fire, sinking one and damaging many others. Rozhdestvensky was wild with rage, but was wise enough to take the lesson of this debacle. He reprimanded those responsible and then ordered intensive battle training for all his crews. The best possible must be achieved, and that was the least Rozhdestvensky demanded. The majority of the Tsar's more seasoned officers and men might well be blockaded at Port Arthur, but he was determined that his crews would be every bit as battle-ready by the time they arrived.

To add to his difficulties Rozhdestvensky also had the problem of refuelling his armada in the months before it reached its destination. Only after much diplomatic wrangling could refuelling take place at Dakar on November 16. But by mid-December the fleet was rounding The Cape of Good Hope and ploughing forward into the Indian Ocean.

Russia decides on battle

News was received towards the end of the year that Port Arthur was falling to the besieging Japanese land forces. The Russian ships there were being slowly destroyed by Admiral Togo's fleet. Relief was not possible any more, for Port Arthur could not last out long enough for it to arrive. Rozhdestvensky therefore analysed and revised his orders. As Port Arthur could not now be relieved, the enemy must be faced in the open sea and the issue decided there.

By March 1905, as he prepared to leave the refuelling port at Madagascar, Rozhdestvensky had decided on this new course of action. He was eager to do battle with Togo now, but, as the

Russian battleships steam towards Tsushima Strait – and disaster. Four new battleships, the flagship Suvarov, Alexander III, Borodino *and* Orel *formed the core of the fleet. All but* Orel *were destroyed.*

fleet was about to set sail, another order was received from St Petersburg. The order instructed Rozhdestvensky to join the Third Pacific Squadron, as this would give him yet more ships for his striking force. What, on the face of it, appeared to be extra help Rozhdestvensky knew to be potentially disastrous. For the Third Pacific Squadron was nothing more than a group of rusting old ships, led mostly by passed-over officers. They would weigh down his fast-moving modern fleet. The ships were not nearly so fast, nor so heavily armed and the men were even less experienced than his own battle fleet.

Rozhdestvensky, however, had no choice, and set sail for Port Arthur in mid-March to rendezvous with his promised reinforcements at Cam Ranh Bay. He pushed his fleet at full speed across the Indian Ocean, through the Malacca Strait, around Singapore, and on to Cam Ranh Bay, arriving on April 14 to join with the squadron of ancient war vessels that awaited him there. The Tsarist fleet now numbered 52 ships.

Admiral Togo was well aware of the coming Tsarist armada. He knew that if he could destroy it, the seas would be wiped completely clear of Russian influence. Imperial Japan would win a momentous victory, and the Divine Navy would reign supreme throughout the waters of the Far East. After the fall of Port Arthur, therefore, Togo rushed his fleet back to Japan for a badly needed overhaul and a complete refitting.

Togo's foresight in doing this now proved its value. Patrols were ordered to scour Tsushima Strait, for Togo was certain that Rozhdestvensky would make his way there. This was because Tsushima Strait lay between Korea and Japan, and Togo was certain that Rozhdestvensky's only possible course was to make for the one remaining port held by the Russians, Vladivostok. The Japanese patrols were to search for the oncoming Tsarist fleet – if the fleet could be sighted soon enough, Admiral Togo could meet it on his own terms, he would have time to place his fleet strategically and, if the divine guidance he sought was with him, annihilate the Russian armada.

First contact

On May 27, 1905, at first light, the Japanese cruiser *Shinano Maru* of the advance patrol

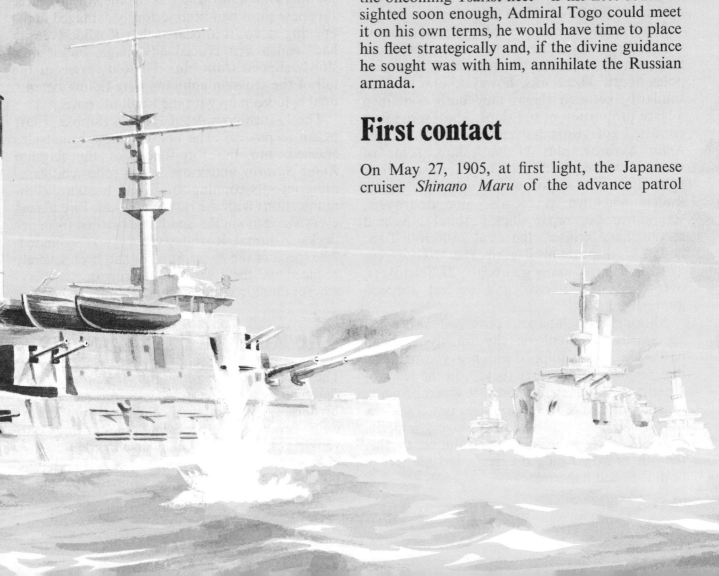

sighted a Russian vessel. The cruiser shadowed for nearly two hours until the light improved sufficiently for it positively to identify at least ten Russian warships. They were sailing in formation into Tsushima Strait, just as Togo had expected. A message was quickly despatched informing the Admiral. Togo knew that the first part of his plans could now be put into action. Admiral Rozhdestvensky was running his armada of 52 vessels right down the Japanese throats!

But the *Shinano Maru* had been spotted, and for his part Rozhdestvensky knew that his own plans had to be revised. He could no longer hope to slip through Tsushima Strait unobserved, so he prepared his fleet for action, and issued the signal 'ammunition not to be wasted' to all of his ships. Manoeuvring his ships into battle formation, he steamed on into the Strait. The Russians had sailed half-way round the world and had waited from October 9, 1904, until now, May 27 of the following year, for this action. Rozhdestvensky was determined to avenge the defeat of Port Arthur and to restore Russian honour. Togo was equally determined to blast the remains of the Russian fleet from the seas.

Shortly after noon on May 27, the battle forces approached one another. On paper both fleets were formidable, but in practice they were poles apart. There was, however, one obvious similarity between them: they both contained a large proportion of old ships. The Tsarist fleet consisted of Rozhdestvensky's flagship, the *Kniaz Suvarov*, plus 11 battleships, some of which were very old, four large cruisers, four light cruisers, two of which acted as flotilla leaders and two as escorts, nine destroyers, several transport repair ships, hospital ships, and an auxiliary cruiser, the *Ural*. Admiral Togo had at his disposal his flagship, the *Mikasa*, plus 27 capital ships, many gun-boats, 21 destroyers, over 70 torpedo-boats and several torpedo gunboats.

Although the Japanese possessed a marked superiority in numbers, the mighty Russian battleships were equipped with heavy armaments that might possibly carry the day in the teeth of the greater Japanese numbers. It was a bringing together of two of the greatest sea powers of the time. Such a clash between two mighty imperial warriors, each with an iron resolution to slay the other, would indeed exact a terrible toll in both lives and material.

Admiral Togo attacks

As the forces slowly closed, the Tsarist fleet was in two columns, in line ahead formation. The Imperial fleet took up a single line ahead disposition. The first move was to fall to Admiral Togo. He decided to attack the Tsarist port column, as this was nearest to the course to Vladivostok and was therefore a possible escape route for the Russians. He also realized that this column contained the weaker, slower ships. He increased speed and crossed the Russian bows five miles in front as he was anxious to prevent the battle developing into a chase which could lead to the escape of a few Russian ships. Togo was confident enough to play for the highest stakes and was determined that the Russians would be staking all or nothing as well.

During the 15 minutes it took the Japanese fleet to complete its manoeuvre, Rozhdestvensky opened fire. Shells ripped into the Japanese armoured cruisers *Yakumo* and *Asama*. The *Asama's* steering gear was badly damaged and she was sent wallowing out of line. In all, three Japanese ships had been seriously damaged in the opening salvo. It appeared that Rozhdestvensky had won a first crucial advantage, but it now slowly slipped from him. The old vessels at the tail of the Russian columns were falling behind, unable to keep up with the headlong pace.

The U-turn completed, Togo's gamble at last began to pay off. The first Japanese broadsides crashed into the fore-funnel of the flagship *Kniaz Suvarov* and more salvos followed, slamming into its conning-tower and breaking communications with the rest of the fleet. Fire blazed everywhere as smoke and flame belched from her decks. Admiral Rozhdestvensky was wounded. The speed of the *Kniaz Suvarov* had been severely reduced and there was smouldering debris everywhere: the ship was in complete disarray.

The Russian flagship sinks

The ships astern, the *Imperator Alexander III* and *Borodino*, were already being engaged by the Japanese. The Imperial Japanese battleships were firing armour-piercing shells, and pulverizing blasts on the *Kniaz Suvarov* tore into her hull. The grey sea poured in through the breaches, the main mast was hurled over and a

Japanese warships open fire on the Russian fleet at the start of the battle. At Tsushima the Russian guns fired first while the Japanese fleet manoeuvred into positions that would ensure a complete victory.

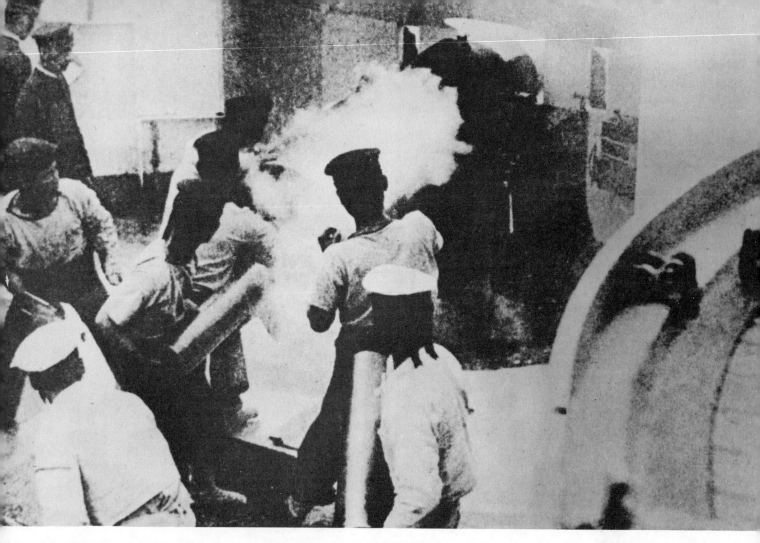

funnel collapsed across the deck, exploding as it crashed down. All authority disappeared from the maimed flagship; and she listed out of control wreathed in smoke and flame.

At a little past seven in the evening, having been reduced to a blazing wreck, the vessel was violently attacked by the Japanese torpedo boats. The wounded Admiral Rozhdestvensky was transferred to the destroyer *Buiny*, which had run alongside the stricken battleship to take off a number of the wounded sailors. The *Kniaz Suvarov* now came in for a tremendous on-slaught. As shells poured into her she staggered, rolled on her side and sank.

Of the five new battleships the *Orel* was the only one now left afloat. The remainder of the Russian fleet was fairing slightly better and, though they had been battered, they were intact. At sundown Togo signalled his triumphant battleships to withdraw leaving the night free for torpedo-boat attacks. Throughout the night these fast little ships dogged the heels of the battered fleet as it made what speed it could for the haven of Vladivostok.

The Divine Wind was indeed blowing for Togo, and he could do no wrong now. Even a parting shot from the battleship *Fuji* found its mark in the *Borodino*. An eye-witness account stated that the *Borodino* immediately burst into flame, and immense clouds of smoke poured from her funnel tops. Her boilers exploded with an ear-shattering roar as dense clouds of smoke and steam billowed high into the air. The *Borodino* went to the bottom with a series of tremendous explosions.

The Japanese torpedo-boats lunged their parry-and-thrust attacks time and time again at the limping Tsarist fleet. So daring were these torpedo-boats' raids that they came at times to within 20 yards of the Russian ships before despatching their cargoes of death and destruction.

As dawn broke on May 28 the remains of the Russian fleet found themselves surrounded by Japanese cruisers. The torpedo-boats had completed their task admirably. Admiral Togo now ordered the cruisers to open fire. They started to pour in rounds of fire while they themselves kept out of range of the remaining old Russian guns.

'We surrender'...

Due to the wounds Rozhdestvensky had received, and his subsequent transfer to the destroyer *Buiny*, an underling, Admiral Nebogatov had assumed command of what was left of the Russian fleet. In the conditions in which he now found himself Nebogatov decided to surrender, being convinced that no more useful purpose would be gained by the sacrifice of the 2,000 men left under his command. They still had 300 miles to go to Vladivostok, and in the circumstances could not possibly make it.

Over 25 Japanese vessels now surrounded the remnants of the once proud Tsarist fleet, and leading them was Admiral Togo's flagship, the *Mikasa*. Admiral Togo had the Russian fleet within his grasp. From the bridge of his flagship Togo slowly savoured the scene. His eyes, scanning every Russian ship in turn, told him all he needed to know. Victory was his. The Russians could not possibly escape.

Admiral Nebogatov's decision weighed heavily. Admiral Rozhdestvensky was lying

Opposite Japanese gunners in action at Tsushima.

Above The 13,500 ton Russian flagship, Suvarov, *starts to sink (foreground). The* Alexander III *blazes in the background before sinking. Both were new battleships.*

unconscious and all his fleet, after so long a journey, were tired and worn out. The Russian ships hauled down their colours and Nebogatov ordered the flag 'XGE', the international code flag for 'we surrender', to be raised. But Admiral Togo was amazed. 'We surrender' was not a message a Japanese officer would ever make and he was deeply worried lest this was a last minute ploy. One of Togo's maxims had always been 'Never fear a strong enemy, and never despise a weak one'.

... but Togo continues fire

What was Togo to do? Let the Tsarist fleet off the hook and 'surrender'? Or do as he had always done, and make completely sure of victory? Togo thought for a few moments and then ordered the big guns of his fleet to blast the Russian ships out of the water. But when the Japanese started bombarding the Russian fleet, and Togo saw the helpless Russian ships with surrender flags at their masts being inevitably battered to death, he took pity on them. He soon had had enough of this obviously one-sided action. With the Russian ships at a standstill he ordered the cease-fire. Togo was to recall, years later, that the Russian decision to surrender was 'utterly beyond our expectations'.

The final reckoning

The Russians had lost all of their battleships, four of their eight cruisers, seven of their nine destroyers, as well as 4,830 officers and men, with over 10,000 wounded or captured. The Japanese had lost only 117 men, with less than a thousand wounded, and two torpedo-boats.

Of the Russian ships that entered Tsushima Strait, all but three had been sunk, captured or interned. These three finally limped out of the clutches of the Imperial Japanese Navy and staggered, miraculously, into Vladisvostok. The captured Russian ships were escorted or towed back to Japan, and the wounded Rozhdestvensky put into a naval hospital. Togo was heaped with honours from his delighted Emperor and was hailed as the greatest sea warrior Japan had ever known. The prize he had won for Japan was nothing less than the foundation of an Empire.

As the weeks slipped by, Admiral Rozhdestvensky slowly recovered his health but time could not restore his spirit. The once proud

Major ships in the Battle of Tsushima Strait

RUSSIAN FLEET

Name	Tonnage	Main Armament		Speed
Kniaz Suvarov* (Flagship)	13,516	4 12in.,	12 6in.	17.6 Knots
Imperator Alexander III*	13,516	4 12in.,	12 6in.	17.6 Knots
Borodino*	13,516	4 12in.,	12 6in.	17.8 Knots
Orel	13,516	4 12in.,	12 6in.	17.6 Knots
Osslyabya*	12,674	4 10in.,	11 6in.	18.3 Knots
Sissoi Veliki*	10,400	4 12in.,	6 6in.	15.7 Knots
Navarin*	10,200	4 12in.,	8 6in.	15.7 Knots
Imperator Nikolai I	9,672	2 12in.,	4 9in.	14.0 Knots
Admiral Nakimov*	8,524	8 8in.,	10 6in.	16.6 Knots
Oleg	6,645	12 6in.		23.0 Knots
Aurora	6,731	8 6in.		20.0 Knots
Dimitri Donskoi*	6,200	6 6in.,	10 4.7in.	16.5 Knots
Vladimir Monomach*	5,593	5 6in.,	6 4.7in.	17.5 Knots
Admiral Senyavin	4,960	4 9.4in.,	4 6in.	16.1 Knots
General Admiral Apraxin	4,126	3 10in.,	4 4.7in.	16.0 Knots
Admiral Ushakov*	4,126	4 9.4in.,	4 6in.	16.1 Knots
Jemtchug	3,103	6 4.7in.		24.0 Knots
Izumrud	3,103	6 4.7in.		24.0 Knots
Almaz	3,285			
Svietlana*	3,828			

* Vessels known to have been sunk

JAPANESE FLEET

Name	Tonnage	Main Armament		Speed
Mikasa (Flagship)	15,140	4 12in.,	14 6in.	18.0 Knots
Asahi	15,200	4 12in.,	14 6in.	18.0 Knots
Shikishima	14,850	4 12in.,	14 6in.	18.0 Knots
Fuji	12,450	4 12in.,	10 6in.	18.0 Knots
Idzumo	9,750	4 8in.,	14 6in.	21.0 Knots
Iwate	9,750	4 8in.,	14 6in.	21.0 Knots
Tokiwa	9,750	4 8in.,	14 6in.	21.5 Knots
Asama	9,700	4 8in.,	14 6in.	21.5 Knots
Yakumo	9,646	4 8in.,	12 6in.	20.0 Knots
Adzuma	9,307	4 8in.,	12 6in.	20.0 Knots
Nisshin	7,628	4 8in.,	14 6in.	20.0 Knots
Kasuga	7,628	1 10in.,	2 8in. 14 6in.	20.0 Knots
Chin-Yen	7,220	4 12in.,	4 6in.	15.0 Knots
Kasagi	4,862	2 8in.,	10 4.7in.	22.5 Knots
Chitose	4,760	2 8in.,	10 4.7in.	22.5 Knots
Itsukushima	4,210	1 12.5in.,	11 4.7in.	16.0 Knots
Hashidate	4,210	1 12.5in.,	11 4.7in.	16.0 Knots
Matsushima	4,210	1 12.5in.,	11 4.7in.	16.0 Knots
Naniwa	3,650	8 6in.,		18.0 Knots
Takichiho	3,650	2 10in.,	6 6in.,	18.0 Knots
Tsushima	3,365	6 6in.		20.0 Knots
Nitaka	3,365	6 6in.		20.0 Knots
Fuso	3,718	4 10in.,	4 6in.	13.0 Knots
Akitsushima	3,150	4 6in.,	6 4.7in.	19.0 Knots
Otawa	3,000	2 6in.,	6 4.7in.	21.0 Knots
Izumi	2,950	2 6in.,	6 4.7in.	17.0 Knots
Akushi	2,657	2 6in.,	6 4.7in.	20.0 Knots
Suma	2,657	2 6in.,	6 4.7in.	20.0 Knots
Chiyoda	2,450	10 4.7in.		19.0 Knots

Masampo Bay in South Korea was Togo's base and from here the attack on the Russians was mounted.
Inset *The Baltic fleet's long voyage to destruction involved a farcical attack on British trawlers.*

Tsushima Strait

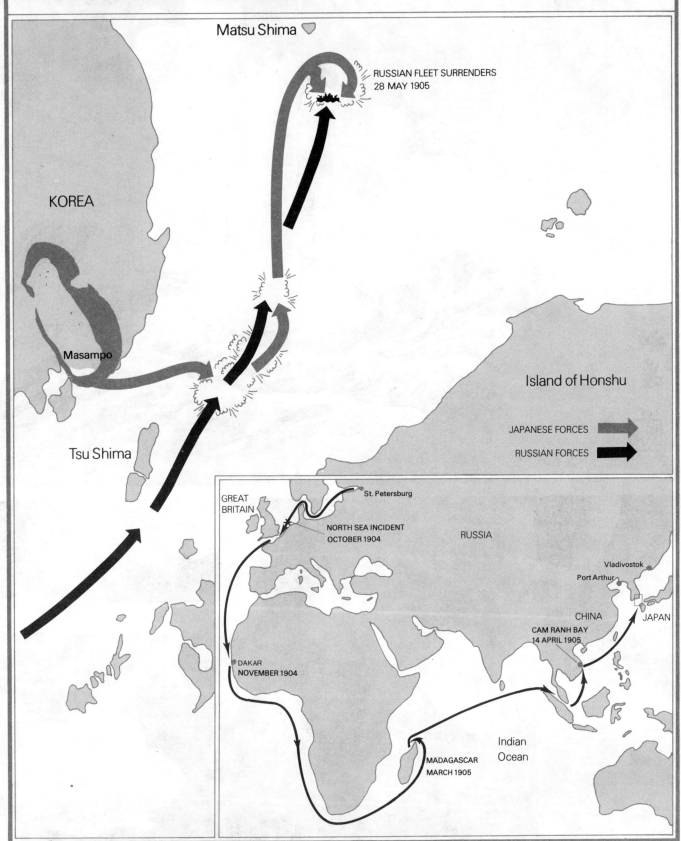

Matsu Shima

RUSSIAN FLEET SURRENDERS
28 MAY 1905

KOREA

Masampo

Island of Honshu

JAPANESE FORCES

RUSSIAN FORCES

Tsu Shima

GREAT
BRITAIN

St. Petersburg

NORTH SEA INCIDENT
OCTOBER 1904

RUSSIA

Vladivostok

Port Arthur

CHINA

JAPAN

CAM RANH BAY
14 APRIL 1905

DAKAR
NOVEMBER 1904

MADAGASCAR
MARCH 1905

Indian
Ocean

Tsarist naval officer was now a broken man. Although Tsar Nicholas II sent him a letter, which thanked him for his services to Russia, he was not to be consoled. Even the now renowned Togo visited him but could not remove the cloud of despair, although he could order that the best medical treatment be given to his adversary. Rozhdestvensky alone realised the gravity of the great disaster that had befallen the once great Russian Navy. The balance of sea power had now swung away from the Tsar and towards Imperial Japan.

Eventually Rozhdestvensky, together with other officers, was allowed to return to St. Petersburg and there the inevitable happened, for a head had to be found on which the blame could be placed. A court martial was held and the verdicts soon reached: Admiral Nebogatov was given the death sentence for surrendering the fleet. Admiral Rozhdetsvensky while not sentenced to death, because he was unconscious at the time, received, for him, an almost equal punishment. He was dismissed from the Service. The Tsar intervened and commuted the death sentence on Nebogatov to life imprisonment. Rozhdestvensky did not live to old age. He died within three years, in 1909, a sad and embittered man.

When Admiral Togo achieved his remarkable victory in Tsushima Strait he had, at one stroke, brought about the emergence of Japan as a massive sea power. This island race was now emerging from its sheltered past into a great future.

Left above *A Japanese print showing a Russian warship sinking during the battle of Tsushima.*

Left *Another print depicts night fighting at Tsushima. Russian searchlights sweep the sea – and light up Russian targets for Japanese torpedo boats.*

JUTLAND

Two mighty fleets met at Jutland in the North Sea in 1916 in what should have been the greatest battle of all time, a test of the British faith in guns and of the German confidence in their new tactics. But both sides were too wary for a decisive engagement.

When war broke out between the British and German Empires in 1914, the world had been in a state of uneasy peace for many years. The all-powerful British Empire had seen with mounting alarm how the confident young German Empire was growing in power and ambition. As the interests of these two great powers clashed in one place after another, it became obvious that the traditional way of settling rivalries between empires would soon be called for. Events following in the wake of the assassination of the Archduke Ferdinand in Sarajevo brought these tensions to a head, and war was declared.

A bloody and dogged struggle for supremacy developed. Germany tried new and often daring tactics on both the land and the sea, whereas the more traditionally-oriented Allies preferred their own well-tried methods.

One such confrontation between the young and venturesome and the old and tried took place in May 1916, around an area known as the Jutland Bank, in the North Sea. The navies amassed by the two Empires were vastly different in character and design. The tactics employed by the Royal Navy were those that had stood the test of time. They were, in fact, similar to those employed by brilliant commanders like Nelson and Rodney in bygone days. The 'single line ahead' battle formation, which relied for its success on accurate and heavy gunfire, was that adopted by the conservative strategists of the Royal Navy.

Guns to smash any enemy

Their ships were all powerfully armed, but carried weak armour. This meant that they were still capable of sustained high speed under battle conditions. It was thought, as it had always been thought, that the powerful armament could completely overwhelm any enemy. The single line ahead formation was considered an arrow flying through the seas, capable of delivering its fire to left or right at an enemy and piercing his set battle lines. The plan was to drive an attack direct straight at the heart of the enemy's fleet.

The German Navy, for its part, had developed its own types of naval strategy. A modern, independent plan of campaign had been devised in the privacy of secret naval exercises in the Baltic

Sea. This relied upon the fleet being broken into small and extremely manoeuvrable squadrons. These squadrons were trained to adopt independent action, in place of the rigid patterns of the massed fleets of the Royal Navy. Individual small fighting squadrons were to carry out raids with lightning speed and precision. These then were the tactics to be employed by the antagonists.

Jellicoe and von Scheer

The British Fleet, known as the Grand Fleet, was led by Commander-in-Chief Admiral Sir John Jellicoe. His opponent was Admiral Reinhard von Scheer. The two men were as different in character and temperament as were their respective fleets. Jellicoe, a trained gunnery officer, placed his faith in the trusted methods of the Royal Navy. He was a man who could bear great burdens with bulldog-like tenacity, a man who was as solid and dependable as the Empire he served.

Von Scheer was a man young in ideas, willing to experiment and even to take risks in order that new methods and inventions might be tried. He realized that his enemy was formidable, and respected that enemy enough to learn from him. He realized, too, that the tactics of the Royal Navy had changed little over the last few decades, and was therefore willing to consider

Top Admiral Sir John Jellicoe, Commander-in-Chief of Britain's Grand Fleet believed in rigid, regimented tactics. **Above** His opponent, Admiral von Scheer, Commander-in-Chief of the German High Sea Fleet, was daring and inventive. At Jutland their fleets waged a bloody struggle. The outcome was inconclusive and the naval balance between the two warring empires remained unchanged. **Below and overleaf** British warships in action.

daring and sometimes foolhardy innovations in battle training. By constantly experimenting with new ideas, he hoped to arrive at a brand of naval warfare that the British Fleet could not counter.

The full-scale confrontation of the two navies was not long in coming. The German Fleet, in a series of brilliantly conceived raids upon the coast of Great Britain, had considerably wounded the pride of the Royal Navy. One such raid, on April 24, 1916, consisted of part of the German complement of battle-cruisers drawing in close to the British coast near Lowestoft and there, for a short while, bombarding the town before retiring at great speed. It took audacity, stemming from the ideas of Admiral von Scheer, to come in so close to the shores of Great Britain and deal such a blow to morale.

Battle Fleets gather

Admiral Jellicoe had gathered his Battle Fleet together at three stations in Scotland: the Firth of Forth, the Moray Forth and Scapa Flow. Shortly after the daring raid on Lowestoft, on May 30, he received a signal that the German High Seas Fleet was massing in strength off Wilhelmshaven. That news was enough to spur Jellicoe into action. He arranged with Vice-Admiral Beatty, the commander of the British battle-cruisers in the Firth of Forth, to rendezvous with him in a position to the south of Norway, near the entrance to the Skagerrak, latitude 57° 45′ North, longitude 04° 15′ East, at 1400 on May 31. After despatching the message to Vice-Admiral Beatty the two halves of the main British Fleet sailed from Scapa Flow and the Moray Forth, linking up at noon to continue their journey together.

About to gather together was one of the biggest fleets of heavily-armed ships that the world had ever seen. There were four Battle Squadrons, the 1st Squadron having as its flagship the Fleet flagship HMS *Iron Duke*, a 25,000-ton battleship

of which the armament consisted of ten 13½-inch guns and 12 six-inch guns. In this 1st Battle Squadron were seven other battleships of equal or comparable size. The 2nd Battle Squadron had as its flagship HMS *King George V*, a 23,000-ton battleship, also with ten 13½-inch guns, and 16 four-inch guns. As well as the *King George V*, the Battle Squadron boasted seven other huge 23,000-ton battleships. The 4th Battle Squadron had at its head HMS *Royal Oak*, a 27,500-ton battleship with eight 14-inch guns and 12 six-inch guns. She was supported by six other similar battleships. The smallest Battle Squadron, the 5th, was led by one of the heaviest battleships in the entire Fleet, HMS *Valiant*, a 27,500-ton vessel with eight 15-inch guns and eight six-inch guns. She was supported by three 27,000-ton battleships.

Admiral Beatty's Battle-cruiser Fleet, which was to join up with Jellicoe's, was a much more flexible array. It consisted of nine battle-cruiser and light cruiser squadrons. HMS *Lion* was Vice-Admiral Beatty's flagship, and also led the 1st Battle-cruiser Squadron. The 26,350-ton *Lion* sported heavy armaments of eight 13.5-inch guns and sixteen four-inch guns. All told, the Battle-cruiser Squadrons and Light-cruiser Squadrons totalled 35 warships. Attached to the massing Fleet was five light-cruisers, three leading flotilla cruisers and over six destroyer flotillas. One seaplane carrier acted as a support.

The German Fleet

The German Fleet was not nearly as large, but all its ships were of fairly recent construction. The Fleet flagship, which headed the 1st German Battle Squadron, was the *Friedrich der Grosse*. This 24,700-ton ship had ten 12-inch guns and fourteen six-inch guns. The 1st Battle Squadron consisted of eight other comparable battleships. The 2nd Battle Squadron was headed by the

Deutschland, a 13,200-ton pre-Dreadnought battleship, with armament of four 11-inch guns and 14 6.7-inch guns. She was joined by five other pre-Dreadnought battleships of the same type. The 3rd Squadron was led by the *Konig*, a 25,390-ton battleship, which was armed with 12-inch guns and 14 six-inch guns. She in turn was supported by six other battleships of the same description. Supplementing these were one Battle-cruiser Squadron of five warships, a Light-cruiser Squadron of nine warships, two cruisers and over six flotilla destroyer squadrons.

These two enormous Fleets covered a huge area of sea. The British Grand Fleet now ranged from horizon to horizon, a vast armada ready to destroy the enemy. The German Fleet had also assembled, and was moving out into the North

Above *Part of the massive firepower that the British Grand Fleet brought to Jutland.*

Below *The* Hercules, *20,000 tons, and the* Invincible, *17,250 tons.* Invincible *was sunk at Jutland.*

Sea with Admiral von Scheer in command. Slowly, and as yet unknown to one another, the two antagonists closed. Surprise was a vital part of Jellicoe's plan, which was to sweep into the Skagerrak and Kattegat with his light-cruisers hoping to flush out the enemy into the jaws of his massed battleships lying in wait outside.

First contacts

HMS *Galatea*, of the 1st Light-cruiser Squadron, made the first sighting of a German ship at 1420 on May 31 and immediately sent signals to Vice-Admiral Beatty and Admiral Jellicoe to inform them. The German warship was the *Elbing*, one of the light cruisers of an advance scouting group. Naturally the *Elbing* also signalled her superiors, and Vice Admiral von Hipper, who commanded the light-cruisers, and Admiral von Scheer were duly informed of the Royal Navy's presence. Slowly the two mighty Fleets manoeuvred into their battle formations.

At 1547, in perfect visibility, the battle cruisers of both Fleets opened fire simultaneously at a range of approximately 16,000 yards. Because of a missed signal, British fire upon the German Fleet was at first uncoordinated. After ten minutes this mistake was rectified, and the British and German Fleets exchanged even fire, ship for ship, blow for blow. But the first advantage had already gone to von Scheer: the British had manoeuvred themselves into a position where they were clearly defined against a western sky. This meant that the German gunners could pick their targets at will. The German commanders, bringing their modern tactics into play, now adopted a less regimented form of attack against the inflexible British formation. No major hits had yet been scored, however, despite the thousands of rounds of ammunition that had been poured into both armadas. Like two heavyweight boxers trading punch for punch, they continued to slog out the battle.

A thousand men go down

At this point the German cruiser *Von der Tann* was engaging her opposite number, HMS *Indefatigable*. The *Indefatigable* was struck by two accurate salvos in quick succession, both of which burst upon her upper deck-work. She exploded in a sheet of flame and sank immediately. Over 1,000 men perished.

At 1625, the Royal Navy suffered another blow: after sinking the *Indefatigable*, the *Von der Tann* had turned her attentions to the 26,000-ton cruiser *Queen Mary*. The precision of the gunners on the German battle-cruiser was demonstrated a second time. An accurate salvo hit the *Queen Mary* and she too immediately exploded and sank, taking with her over 1,250 men.

The 5th Battle Squadron finally managed to come within firing range. Closing at a rate of some 25 knots, they started a bombardment of the German ships. The initial advantage was slowly slipping from von Scheer, and he thought about breaking off the action and retiring quickly after his two successes. The 5th Battle Squadron had other ideas and the battle went on as furiously as ever.

The German squadrons were now independently attacking the massive Grand Fleet. During one of these sallies Admiral von Hipper directed his fire against the weaker destroyer flotillas and the destroyers *Nestor* and *Nomad* were severely mauled and left almost awash, wallowing helplessly. Von Scheer ordered his battleships to finish them off and the destroyers were sunk by gunfire delivered at point-blank range.

Battle-cruiser Lion, *Admiral Beatty's flagship and leader of the 1st Battle-cruiser Squadron. The 26,350-ton* Lion, *which carried eight 13.5-inch guns and 16 four-inch guns, took a heavy pounding in the battle despite its nine-inch armour.*

The Grand Fleet attempted to maintain its rigid disciplined lines, with von Scheer trying as many shifts of tactics as he could. The two battle-ships HMS *Barham* and HMS *Malaya* were now in disarray after suffering several concentrated attacks. On the German side, the *Konig* had received a severe battering and was almost put out of action.

Smoke blots out the sun

Fighting was taking place over a wide area of sea. By this time, the smoke had almost blotted out the light of the sun. For miles and miles around the air was thick with the smell of cordite. But still the battle raged. Concentrated fire upon the German Second Scouting Group was rewarded when the Royal Navy's battle-cruisers sank the

Below Smoke billows from the 26,000 ton cruiser Queen Mary *as she sinks with her 1000 strong crew. She carried eight 15-inch guns. Her killer, the* Von der Tann *also sank the* Indefatigable.

Right The 24,600 ton German cruiser Seydlitz *shrouded in smoke after scuttling at Jutland.*

4,900-ton light-cruiser *Wiesbaden*, but the British lost the destroyer *Shark*. The armoured-cruiser HMS *Defence*, after being attacked by German battle-cruisers, exploded and sank immediately with her complement of 900 men. The cruiser HMS *Warrior*, astern of the *Defence*, also came in for heavy punishment and was extensively damaged. She rode out the attack, but could not be of any further use to Jellicoe that day. Two of the German battle-cruisers hauled out of their line, so fierce was one particular engagement with the British 3rd Battle-cruiser Squadron. The *Konig* was completely aflame by now, but on the British side, the *Invincible* was hit near her magazines and exploded in a sheet of blinding flame, sinking with the loss of 1,000 men.

The battle was now approaching its final phase: the British had, as far as possible, maintained their stations, but had taken enormous punishment. The advantage swayed to and fro. First von Scheer, then Jellicoe appeared to take a lead. At about 1900, as the mist began to come up and reduce the already deteriorating visibility even further, von Scheer started his last attack. He knew he had gained more than he had lost, and was ready to withdraw gracefully as soon as he had delivered one more blow. He was determined, in the failing light, to deliver a body blow

to the very heart of the British Grand Fleet. He ordered his battle-cruisers to charge at will the highly disciplined formation of the British Fleet. But what was to be a body blow turned out to be a near disaster.

The German 'death ride'

As soon as the German battle-cruisers came into range, Jellicoe's guns delivered a highly concentrated and efficient barrage which von Scheer's battle-cruisers had no choice but to run. This charge became known later as the 'death ride'. The accuracy of the British fire brought the German warships to a virtual halt and seeing that the body blow could not be delivered, von Scheer ordered his battered cruisers to turn away under the cover of a smoke screen. They soon disappeared from Jellicoe's sight into the fading light. Jellicoe would not be drawn into following the fleeing German ships. He was later to say that he had thought von Scheer's intention was to draw the British over strategically-laid mines. He declined to risk his ships in such a pursuit.

With the disappearance of the German cruisers the main engagements came to an end. A sudden silence came upon the battered Fleets which were shrouded in smoke and mist as well as the darkness of night. The cloak of darkness, however, was to prove a mixed blessing to both sides. Admiral Jellicoe ordered his ships back into line, but not to show too many lights lest these should give away their positions to any lurking or stray German warship. Von Scheer gave the same order: the two battle fleets were both trying to regroup, groping their way sightlessly in an inky darkness. Chance meetings were bound to happen, and they were not long in coming.

The first disaster came to the cruiser HMS *Black Prince*. While endeavouring to rejoin her squadron, she blundered into the retreating German warships. The *Black Prince* was recognized, fired upon and sunk in one swift action before she had any chance of escape. She took over 850 men to a watery grave. The German battleship *Pommern* was caught without guard and attacked by the Royal Navy's 12th Destroyer Flotilla. She was sunk by torpedo, 'blown to atoms' according to eye-witness accounts.

The battle peters out

Admiral Jellicoe re-grouped throughout the night in an attempt to manoeuvre his vast Fleet into a

position between the German coastline and where he calculated the German Fleet to be. When daylight broke he was convinced that his ships now lay ready to catch the retreating von Scheer as he slipped back to port. Hour after hour Jellicoe waited, scanning the horizon for the remains of von Scheer's squadrons. Shortly after 1430, after some ten hours of waiting, he received a signal from the Admiralty informing him that the German Fleet had evaded him, and was now back in its own ports. Admiral Jellicoe turned his fleet homeward to Scapa Flow. The Battle of Jutland had come to an end.

The battle itself was indecisive, for neither side suffered complete defeat. This did not stop it being considered a severe blow to morale by both nations. Although Jellicoe earned considerable respect for the discipline that had been apparent throughout his Fleet, he came in for criticism. He had lost three battle-cruisers, three cruisers and seven destroyers, against the German loss of one battleship, one cruiser, two destroyers and four light-cruisers. Over 6,000 men of the Royal Navy had been lost, as against the German casualties of 3,000. Jellicoe was forced in the days to come to ask himself why the battle had not been decisive, and why his rigid, regimented tactics had not won the day. It was later accepted that a 'strategic' victory had, in fact, been achieved, for the German Fleet was never again to put to sea in such large numbers. For von Scheer, the battle had valuable lessons. He had endeavoured to use modern and untried tactics, but these had only been partially successful. He in turn was to re-think his battle strategy.

The slogging heavyweight contest had proved little, other than that the combatants had lost 21 ships and 9,823 men. This was a tremendous price to pay for an indecisive outcome: the naval balance of power between the two nations remained unchanged. Indeed, the lesson of Jutland can virtually serve as the lesson of World War I. For all the heroism and suffering of both sides, in the end too many men had perished for very little.

Major ships in the Battle of Jutland

BRITISH FLEET:

1st Battle Squadron:

Name	Tonnage	Main Armament		Speed
Iron Duke (Flagship)	25,000	10 13.5in.,	12 6in.	21 Knots
Agincourt	27,500	14 12in.,	20 6in.	22 Knots
Colossus	20,000	10 12in.,	16 4in.	21 Knots
Hercules	20,000	10 12in.,	16 4in.	21 Knots
Marlborough	25,000	10 13.5in.,	12 6in.	21 Knots
Neptune	19,900	10 12in.,	16 4in.	21 Knots
Revenge	25,750	8 15in.,	12 6in.	22 Knots
St Vincent	19,250	10 12in.,	16 4in.	21 Knots

2nd Battle Squadron:

Name	Tonnage	Main Armament		Speed
King George V	23,000	10 13.5in.,	16 4in.	22 Knots
Ajax	23,000	10 13.5in.,	16 4in.	22 Knots
Centurion	23,000	10 13.5in.,	16 4in.	22 Knots
Conqueror	22,500	10 13.5in.,	16 4in.	21 Knots
Erin	23,000	10 13.5in.,	16 6in.	21 Knots
Monarch	22,500	10 13.5in.,	16 4in.	21 Knots
Orion	22,500	10 13.5in.,	16 4in.	21 Knots
Thunderer	22,500	10 13.5in.,	16 4in.	21 Knots

4th Battle Squadron:

Name	Tonnage	Main Armament		Speed
Royal Oak	25,750	8 15in.,	12 6in.	22 Knots
Bellerophon	18,600	10 12in.,	16 4in.	21 Knots
Benbow	25,000	10 13.5in.,	12 6in.	21 Knots
Canada	28,000	10 14in.,	16 6in.	23 Knots
Superb	18,600	10 12in.,	16 4in.	21 Knots
Temeraire	18,600	10 12in.,	16 4in.	21 Knots
Vanguard	19,250	10 12in.,	18 4in.	21 Knots

5th Battle Squadron:

Name	Tonnage	Main Armament		Speed
Valiant	27,500	8 15in.,	8 6in.	25 Knots
Barham	27,500	8 15in.,	12 6in.	25 Knots
Malaya	27,500	8 15in.,	12 6in.	25 Knots
Warspite	27,500	8 15in.,	8 6in.	25 Knots

1st Battle-cruiser Squadron:

Name	Tonnage	Main Armament		Speed
Lion (Flagship)	26,350	8 15in.,	16 4in.	28 Knots
Princess Royal	26,350	8 15in.,	16 4in.	28 Knots
Queen Mary*	26,350	8 15in.,	16 4in.	28 Knots
Tiger	27,000	8 15in.,	12 6in.	28 Knots

2nd Battle-cruiser Squadron:

Name	Tonnage	Main Armament		Speed
Indefatigable*	18,750	8 12in.,	16 4in.	26 Knots
New Zealand	18,750	8 12in.,	16 4in.	27 Knots

3rd Battle-cruiser Squadron:

Name	Tonnage	Main Armament		Speed
Indomitable	17,250	8 12in.,	16 4in.	28 Knots
Inflexible	17,250	8 12in.,	16 4in.	28 Knots
Invincible*	17,250	8 12in.,	16 4in.	28 Knots

1st Cruiser Squadron:

Name	Tonnage	Main Armament		Speed
Black Prince*	13,550	6 9.2in.,	10 6in.	22 Knots
Defence*	14,600	4 9.2in.,	10 7.5in.	21 Knots
Duke of Edinburgh	13,550	6 9.2in.,	10 6in.	22 Knots
Warrior*	13,550	6 9.2in.,	4 7.5in.	22 Knots

The 27,500 ton Warspite *at Jutland.*
Warspite *and her sister ships of the*
Queen Elizabeth class were super-
dreadnoughts, the finest capital ships of
their day.

2nd Cruiser Squadron:

Name	Tonnage	Main Armament		Speed
Cochrane	13,550	6 9.2in.,	4 7.5in.	22 Knots
Hampshire	10,850	4 7.5in.,	6 6in.	22 Knots
Minotaur	14,600	4 9.2in.,	10 .75in.	21 Knots
Shannon	14,600	4 9.2in.,	10 7.5in.	21 Knots

Light Cruisers:

Name	Tonnage	Main Armament		Speed
Active	3,440	10 6in.,		25 Knots
Bellona	3,300	6 4in.		25 Knots
Birmingham	5,400	9 6in.		25 Knots
Birkenhead	5,250	10 5.5in.		25 Knots
Blanche	3,350	10 6in.		25 Knots
Boadicea	3,300	6 4in.		25 Knots
Calliope	3,800	2 6in.,	8 4in.	30 Knots
Canterbury	3,750	5 6in.,		29 Knots
Caroline	3,800	2 6in.,	8 4in.	30 Knots
Castor	3,750	5 6in.,		29 Knots
Champion	3,520	2 6in.,	6 4in.	30 Knots
Chester	5,250	10 5.5in.		26 Knots
Comus	3,800	2 6in.,	8 4in.	30 Knots
Constance	3,800	2 6in.,	8 4in.	30 Knots
Cordelia	3,800	2 6in.,	8 4in.	30 Knots
Dublin	5,400	8 6in.,		25 Knots
Falmouth	5,250	8 6in.		25 Knots
Fearless	3,440	10 4in.		25 Knots
Galatea	3,520	2 6in.,	6 4in.	30 Knots
Gloucester	4,800	2 6in.,	10 4in.	25 Knots
Inconstant	3,520	2 6in.,	6 4in.	30 Knots
Nottingham	5,400	9 6in.		25 Knots
Phaeton	3,520	2 6in.,	6 4in.	30 Knots
Royalist	3,520	2 6in.,	6 4in.	30 Knots
Southampton	5,400	8 6in.		25 Knots
Yarmouth	5,250	8 6in.		25 Knots

Destroyer Flotillas: 1st, 4th, 9th, 10th, 11th, 12th, 13th

(7 Destroyers lost)

GERMAN FLEET:

1st Battle Squadron:

Name	Tonnage	Main Armament		Speed
Friedrich der Grosse (Flagship)	24,700	10 12in.,	14 6in.	20 Knots
Heligoland	22,800	12 12in.,	14 5.9in.	21 Knots
Nassau	18,900	12 11in.,	12 5.9in.	20 Knots
Oldenburg	22,800	12 12in.,	14 5.9in.	21 Knots
Ostfriesland	22,800	12 12in.,	14 5.9in.	21 Knots
Posen	18,900	12 11in.,	12 5.9in.	20 Knots
Rheinland	18,900	12 11in.,	12 5.9in.	20 Knots
Thuringen	22,800	12 12in.,	14 5.9in.	21 Knots
Westfalen	18,900	12 11in.,	12 5.9in.	20 Knots

2nd Battle Squadron:

Name	Tonnage	Main Armament		Speed
Deutschland	13,200	4 11in.,	14 6.7in.	18 Knots
Hannover	13,200	4 11in.,	14 6.7in.	18 Knots
Hessen	13,200	4 11in.,	14 6.7in.	18 Knots

2nd Battle Squadron: (continued)

Name	Tonnage	Main Armament		Speed
Pommern*	13,200	4 11in.,	14 6.7in.	18 Knots
Schlesen	13,200	4 11in.,	14 6.7in.	18 Knots
Schleswig-Holstein	13,200	4 11in.,	14 6.7in.	18 Knots

3rd Battle Squadron:

Name	Tonnage	Main Armament		Speed
König	25,390	10 12in.,	14 5.9in.	22 Knots
Grosser Kurfurst	25,390	10 12in.,	14 5.9in.	22 Knots
Kaiser	24,380	10 12in.,	14 5.9in.	21 Knots
Kaiserin	24,380	10 12in.,	14 5.9in.	21 Knots
Kronprinz Wilhelm	25,390	10 12in.,	14 5.9in.	22 Knots
Markgraf	25,390	10 12in.,	14 5.9in.	22 Knots
Prinzregent Luitpold	24,380	10 12in.,	14 5.9in.	21 Knots

Battle-Cruiser Squadron:

Name	Tonnage	Main Armament		Speed
Derfelinger	26,600	8 12in.,	12 5.9in.	28 Knots
Lutzow*	26,600	8 12in.,	12 5.9in.	28 Knots
Moltke	22,640	10 11in.,	12 5.9in.	27 Knots
Seydlitz	24,610	10 11in.,	12 5.9in.	27 Knots
Von der Tann	19,400	8 11in.,	10 5.9in.	25 Knots

Light Cruisers

Name	Tonnage	Main Armament	Speed
Elbing*	4,320	8 5.9in.	28 Knots
Frankfurt	4,900	7 5.9in.	28 Knots
Frauenlob*	2,715	10 4.1in.	22 Knots
Hamburg	3,250	10 4.1in.	23 Knots
Muenchen	3,250	10 4.1in.	23 Knots
Pillau	4,320	8 5.9in.	28 Knots
Regensburg	4,900	12 4.1in.	28 Knots
Rostock*	4,900	12 4.1in.	28 Knots
Stettin	3,450	10 4.1in.	24 Knots
Stuttgart	3,450	10 4.1in.	24 Knots
Wiesbaden*	4,900	7 5.9in.	28 Knots

Destroyer Flotillas: 1st, 2nd, 3rd, 5th, 6th, 7th, 9th

(2 destroyers lost)

* *Vessels known to have been lost.*

Leading up to the Battle of Jutland, Beatty's Battle-cruisers sailed from the Firth of Forth, Jellicoe's Battleships from the Moray Firth and Scapa Flow. The engagement was indecisive because neither commander could take the risk of fully committing his ships. During the night the German fleet slipped past Jellicoe to regain the safety of their own ports.

Jutland

Faeroe Is.

NORWAY

Shetland Is.

Orkney Is.   *Scapa Flow*

Moray Firth

Firth of Forth

Skagerrak

Kattergat

Jutland Bank

DENMARK

North Sea

GREAT BRITAIN

Wilhelmshaven

Lowestoft

GERMANY

BRITISH FORCES

GERMAN FORCES

MERCHANT CRUISER AT BAY

Against the odds was an understatement when the merchant cruiser Rawalpindi, armed with six-inch guns, met the Scharnhorst *and* Gneisenau, *Hitler's most up to date battleships, with their 11-inch guns. But bravery defiantly did what it could ....*

Silent and deadly, the single torpedo streaked through the dark Atlantic waters towards its unsuspecting prey, the 13,500 ton passenger ship, *Athenia*. Seconds later the torpedo ripped into the port side of the ship, giving the startled passengers and crew the first horrible realization of disaster and announcing to the world that the desperate struggle for mastery of the seas in World War II had begun.

The *Athenia*, a passenger liner of the Donald-

Merchant cruiser at bay

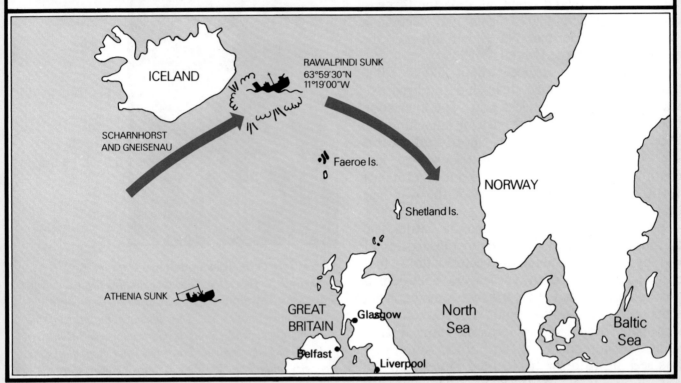

ICELAND

RAWALPINDI SUNK
63°59'30"N
11°19'00"W

SCHARNHORST
AND GNEISENAU

Faeroe Is.

NORWAY

Shetland Is.

ATHENIA SUNK

GREAT
BRITAIN

Glasgow

North
Sea

Baltic
Sea

Belfast

Liverpool

Above The Rawalpindi's *gallant stand against the pride of Hitler's Kriegsmarine occured as the German battleships headed for the Baltic.*

Below The Scharnhorst's *huge guns fire on the* Rawalpindi. Scharnhorst *and her sister ship* Gneisenau *were fast 26,000 ton battle-cruisers, each armed with nine 11-inch guns.* Rawalpindi, *a 17,000 ton merchant ship hastily armed with eight six-inch guns to counter the U-boat threat, was no match for the German warships.*

son Atlantic Line, had left Glasgow on Friday September 1, 1939 at about noon on a voyage, via Liverpool and Belfast, to Montreal. On the evening of September 3, the liner was some 250 miles west of Ireland when, at 1945 the torpedo crashed into her. The *Athenia* had become a victim of the German Navy, her attacker the deadly predator, the U-boat.

The submarine surfaced about 800 to 1,000 yards from the maimed steamship and fired two shells at the ship's wireless gear. The liner soon began to list, making the task of launching the lifeboats extremely difficult. Shortly afterwards the *Athenia* slipped beneath the waves. Her death toll was announced as 128 out of a total of 1,418. The first merchant ship of the war had been lost.

The aftermath was a propaganda battle. The Germans, it seemed had broken the articles of war by sinking a merchant vessel without first ensuring the safety of the passengers. They denied this, claiming that the *Athenia* was carrying arms and ammunition and was, therefore, a legitimate target. The Germans claimed that Winston Churchill, First Lord of the Admiralty, was seeking to draw the United States into the war by provoking an attack on a merchant ship carrying arms, and then claiming that no arms were aboard. Churchill denied this.

Above Hero of the Rawalpindi *was Captain E. C. Kennedy RN. When the German warships fired a warning shot at the* Rawalpindi *Kennedy ordered his meagre six-inch guns to open fire. They blazed in magnificent but futile defiance. Shells from the German warships' massive guns thundered a reply and the brave merchant ship sank. Kennedy and all but 37 of the 302-strong crew were killed.*

Below Rawalpindi *in dock before her fateful voyage. One of her six-inch guns is visible before the bridge.*

Against the odds

The sinking soon highlighted the fact that German submarines had now declared a war of attrition against any British vessel, be it merchant ship or warship. The merchant ships on their peaceful errands had now come under the

The prodigious guns of the Scharnhorst. *The lower guns are 11-inchers and the upper guns are part of the ship's battery of 12 5.9-inch weapons.*

scourge of the Swastika. So devastating was the onslaught against British merchant ships, that 21 vessels were lost in the first couple of weeks of the war. Germany was openly violating international law with these violent acts. 'Sink at sight' with no warning was now common German policy and practice.

By November 1939 the British merchant fleet was starting to be equipped with meagre anti-submarine and anti-aircraft guns for protection. The German press immediately claimed that this 'heavy' armament meant that merchant ships were now auxiliary cruisers. If not before, the German naval forces could now sink them without fear of recrimination!

The beautiful liner *Rawalpindi* was one of the ships converted into an armed merchant cruiser. This 16,700 tons gross steamship was one of four sister ships requisitioned by the Admiralty from their owners, the Peninsular and Oriental Steam Navigation Company, the P & O, for war service. The *Rawalpindi*, launched in 1925, was one of the most elegant liners afloat and the pride of her owners.

Captain E. C. Kennedy commanded the *Rawalpindi*, and the crew was drawn from the ranks of the Royal Navy Reserve, the Royal Naval Volunteer Reserve and Reservists of the Royal Navy. These men were excellent and enthusiastic seamen, but they were given neither the arms nor the type of ship in which to be an effective fighting force.

At the beginning of November 1939 the Admiralty had ordered the *Rawalpindi* to be attached to the Northern patrol, south-east of Iceland. The patrol acted as a lookout and reported the movements of the German Navy in that area. As the elegant *Rawalpindi* first patrolled the cold dark waters of Iceland they were empty – but only for a time. Into the dark seas came an even darker enemy.

Sink at sight

Two German battleships slithered into the liner's view, modern 26,000 ton fighting machines with tremendous armaments, capable of delivering

Death hangs over the Rawalpindi *as smoke and flame billow from her decks. Her crew kept fighting until every gun was out of action and the ship ablaze.*

The 11-inch guns of the Gneisenau *thunder out a salvo, photographed from her sister ship, the* Scharnhorst.

violent destruction from their 11-inch guns. They were the *Scharnhorst* and the *Gneisenau*, the prize battleships of the German fleet and the most up-to-date fighting machines of their class in the world.

After carrying out unrestricted warfare in the Atlantic Ocean the mighty battleships were returning to the Baltic, and home. Passing south-east of Iceland on the afternoon of November 3 they came into view of the *Rawalpindi* and were sighted at 1530.

The armament allocated to the *Rawalpindi* – eight meagre six-inch guns – was no match for the 11-inch guns of the German battleships. Immediately Captain Kennedy realized that the lamb had strayed into the path of the tigers. Not only was he facing vessels built for war, but the odds were two-to-one against him.

On identifying his adversaries, Captain Kennedy ordered that a smoke screen be put up. The smoke screen was laid as quickly as possible to cover an escape he hoped to achieve into a fog bank on the *Rawalpindi*'s port bow. But the lamb had been seen. The *Scharnhorst*, anticipating a possible escape, increased speed and intercepted the *Rawalpindi*'s escape route. A signal ordering Captain Kennedy to stop was sent from the *Scharnhorst* and a shot fired across her bows in warning. This action was followed at 1545 by a salvo from the 11-inch guns at a range of approximately 10,000 yards, for the *Rawalpindi* had ignored the warning.

A lamb to the slaughter

Captain Kennedy quickly ordered open fire and the *Rawalpindi*'s four starboard six-inch guns burst into splendid defiant action. Amazed that a liner, armed with such meagre weapons, should defy the might of the German Navy, the battleships quickly replied. Their third and fourth salvos burst open the *Rawalpindi*. The lamb was being slaughtered. The electric winches of the ammunition supply were destroyed and all the lights put out, the bridge was shot away and the wireless room destroyed, killing nearly everyone stationed there. Death now hung over the proud liner. The *Gneisenau* scored a hit on the starboard battery and immediately put it out of action. Smoke and flame billowed from the *Rawalpindi*'s decks. The enemy battleships had the once majestic liner at their mercy, but the gallant *Rawalpindi* continued to fight until every gun was out of action and the ship ablaze. A pall of fire and smoke cloaked the great and once beautiful liner.

The enemy ceased fire to allow lifeboats to be lowered. The fire had now taken a massive grip and the liner was ablaze from bow to stern. The action had lasted approximately 40 minutes. In that short time the battle of completely unequal adversaries and of tremendous gallantry and bravery by Captain Kennedy and his crew was over. Two of the three boats which were lowered were picked up by the Germans, and the third was picked up later by the *Chitral*, another auxiliary cruiser and also a P & O liner.

The end of the Rawalpindi

Slowly, as if reluctant to die, the *Rawalpindi* slipped under the waves and the seas closed over her. Her 39 officers, including Captain Kennedy, and 226 ratings perished along with their ship. Only 37 seamen survived. The *Scharnhorst* and *Gneisenau* had completed their grim task and continued their broken journey homeward, homeward to the Baltic.

The *Rawalpindi* was the first armed merchant cruiser to be sunk during the war. It was clear that merchant ships with meagre armaments were no match for powerful warships and if the tenuously stretched life-supporting convoys from the Americans were to be maintained something more positive had to be done. A scheme was devised to patrol the break-out areas for the German warships from their home ports, in the Baltic, into the North Atlantic by the warships of the Royal Navy and the aircraft of Coastal Command and not by the poorly equipped armed merchant ships. Then fire could be met with fire.

But the gallant spirit of Captain Kennedy and his crew was not forgotten. Captain Kennedy was himself awarded, posthumously, the Victoria Cross, the nation's highest award for bravery, a fitting reward for an inspiring act of defiance.

Ships in the Merchant cruiser action

Rawalpindi (Armed merchant cruiser)	*Launched:*	March 26, 1925
	Tonnage:	16,697 gross
	Dimensions:	length 548ft. beam 71ft. draught 28ft.
	Speed:	17 knots
	Main armament:	8 6in.
	Complement:	302
Scharnhorst (Battleship)	*Launched:*	October 3, 1936
	Tonnage:	26,000 displacement
	Dimensions:	length 741ft. beam 98ft. draught 25ft.
	Speed:	(designed) 27 knots, (actual) 29 knots
	Main armament:	9 11in. 12 5.9in.
	Complement:	1,461
Gneisenau (Battleship)	*Launched:*	8.12.1936
	Other details identical to Scharnhorst	

DEATH OF THE BISMARCK

A single German ship attempting to reach the open spaces of the Atlantic in 1941 took on the British Navy — and only just lost. In her dash for freedom, the Bismarck *sank the* Hood, *fought many others and almost slipped clear before she was finally caught.*

During April and May of 1941 Grand Admiral Raeder, the outstanding strategist for the German Third Reich, conceived a plan to destroy the convoy system that was keeping Britain alive – and bring Britain nearer to capitulation. The plan consisted of a simultaneous breakout from the Baltic ports and from Brest of the capital ships of German Navy which would then rendezvous in the North Atlantic and, at will, destroy the convoys one by one. The plan also involved five tankers with two supply ships and two reconnaissance ships to support this force. The breakout was code named 'Exercise Rhine' or '*Rheinubung*' and was originally planned to take place in the second half of April when the new moon would

Bismarck, *the newest of Germany's capital ships, threatened to sever Britain's convoy lifeline. In a deadly game of hide-and-seek the older ships of the Royal Navy scoured the northern waters for the* Bismarck *– and sank the pride of the German Navy.*

give dark nights for the breakout.

The Royal Navy was well aware of the tenuous life lines that brought food, oil, munitions; vital materials all needed to keep Britain alive. Realizing the real danger of letting these convoy routes fall to the mercy of the enemy, the British Admiralty made plans to counteract any such act. The Denmark Strait, the main highway into the North Atlantic for any protagonist, was patrolled by the limited forces of the Royal Navy.

Germany's mighty warship

The stage was set for drama. Would the sword of Damocles, in the shape of the new and mighty warships of the German Navy, fall? In falling, would it crush the older and weaker forces of the Royal Navy – put to death the vital, weakly armed, cargo ships – and cut the main life arteries to Britain?

Fate, however, was nibbling at Admiral Raeder's plans. Of the capital ships at his disposal, the modern 10,000 ton heavy cruiser *Prinz Eugen* had been partially damaged by a magnetic mine

in the Baltic. The 26,000 ton battleship *Gneisenau*, built in 1936, was torpedoed by Coastal Command aircraft and extensively damaged. And her sister ship the *Scharnhorst*, also built in 1936, was having an untimely refit which was taking longer than estimated and she had to be ruled out for any immediate plans. The *Bismarck*, however, launched in 1939 and the most powerful warship under Raeder's control, the deadly weapon that bore the name of the founder and First Chancellor of the German Empire, was ready.

Because of these unexpected events the whole breakout operation had to be postponed until the middle of May. Admiral Raeder had set his heart on Exercise Rhine and was determined to see it through. A stranglehold had to be put on Britain if Germany was to emerge victorious.

Bismarck sets out

The damage to the *Prinz Eugen* was repaired as quickly as possible; so she sailed together with Admiral Lutjens in the *Bismarck* after dark on May 18 from the Baltic port of Gdynia to start Exercise Rhine. But fate was against Admiral Raeder. On May 21 a pilot in a Coastal Command photo-reconnaissance Spitfire searching the Norwegian coastline, sighted and photographed, while on routine patrol, two warships in a secluded fiord. One of the warships was identified as the *Bismarck* the other as a cruiser, which later was discovered to be the *Prinz Eugen*. British Intelligence realized from this photograph that the breakout had begun. Sir John Tovey, the Commander in Chief of the Home Fleet, at once sent the battle cruiser HMS *Hood* and her squadron to try and locate and destroy these ships.

Though *Hood* had been built in 1918 her eight 15-inch guns were thought to be the right instruments for inflicting destruction upon the modern German warships. Might would prove right was the British Admiralty's thought.

On May 22 Admiral Tovey received further aerial reconnaissance reports that the *Bismarck* and *Prinz Eugen* were no longer in the fiord. Action had to be taken immediately. The 13-year-old cruiser HMS *Norfolk*, which was already on patrol in the Denmark Strait, was reinforced by sending an older cruiser, the 15-year-old HMS *Suffolk*.

Captain R. M. Ellis, Commanding Officer of the *Suffolk*, had had a very exhausting 48 hours

Opposite 'I shall have to sacrifice myself sooner or later ... I am determined to execute the task which has been entrusted to me in an honourable manner.' Thus Admiral Gunther Lutjens, commander of Exercise Rhine, summed up his task. Lutjens had hoped to postpone the operation until other German capital ships were ready.

Below The 50,000 ton Bismarck, as seen from the Prinz Eugen, 17,000 tons. Exercise Rhine was ill-fated from the start since neither Gneisenau nor Scharnhorst was ready in time for the operation.

for, on the evening of May 23, he had been on duty all that day, the night before and the night before that. The atmospheric conditions where *Suffolk* was searching were unusual; for in the Denmark Strait at this time the visibility was clear over and close to the ice but misty between the ice and the land. *Suffolk* was taking advantage of this, keeping close to the edge of the mist so as to be close to cover if the *Bismarck* were sighted at close range.

Suffolk sights Bismarck

At 1922 a look-out from the *Suffolk* sighted the *Bismarck* closely followed by the *Prinz Eugen* seven miles on the starboard quarter steaming the same course as herself. Captain Ellis immediately forgot his fatigue and made an enemy report signal to Admiral Holland in *Hood*. He then increased the speed of *Suffolk* and altered course to take cover in the mist. Manoeuvring with extreme skill in the mist, and keeping the *Bismarck* under constant radar contact he allowed

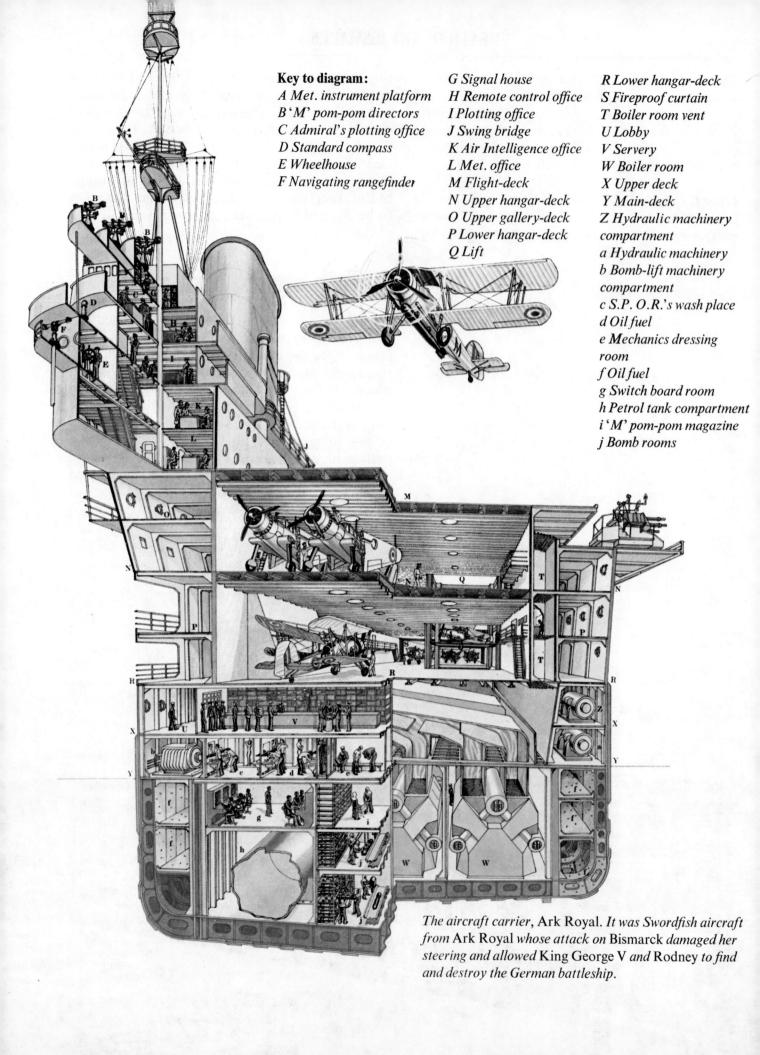

Key to diagram:
A Met. instrument platform
B 'M' pom-pom directors
C Admiral's plotting office
D Standard compass
E Wheelhouse
F Navigating rangefinder
G Signal house
H Remote control office
I Plotting office
J Swing bridge
K Air Intelligence office
L Met. office
M Flight-deck
N Upper hangar-deck
O Upper gallery-deck
P Lower hangar-deck
Q Lift
R Lower hangar-deck
S Fireproof curtain
T Boiler room vent
U Lobby
V Servery
W Boiler room
X Upper deck
Y Main-deck
Z Hydraulic machinery compartment
a Hydraulic machinery
b Bomb-lift machinery compartment
c S.P. O.R.'s wash place
d Oil fuel
e Mechanics dressing room
f Oil fuel
g Switch board room
h Petrol tank compartment
i 'M' pom-pom magazine
j Bomb rooms

The aircraft carrier, Ark Royal. *It was Swordfish aircraft from* Ark Royal *whose attack on* Bismarck *damaged her steering and allowed* King George V *and* Rodney *to find and destroy the German battleship.*

her to pass. At 2028 the *Suffolk* again made visual contact with the enemy, again reported their positions and once more retired into the gathering mists. At the same time *Norfolk* had been closing towards *Suffolk* and also made contact with the *Bismarck*. This time *Bismarck* was on the alert and the very first exchanges of the running battle took place. *Bismarck's* salvos were fairly accurate but *Norfolk* retired unscathed under a smoke screen. So accurate had been the opening salvos from *Bismarck* that large splinters were thrown on board from the shells exploding in the water.

The engagement had been short; *Norfolk* with *Suffolk* had now sought the sanctuary of the mist and were shadowing well behind the enemy. The weather was deteriorating but the pursuit continued. *Norfolk* and *Suffolk* continued the shadowing; awaiting the arrival of the heavy guns of *Hood* in order to try and stop the *Bismarck* and *Prinz Eugen* attempting the break out into the North Atlantic. Through the half-light of the Arctic night, through the mists, through the snow squalls and rain, the pursuit continued.

Hood had not been idle since she received the first enemy report from *Norfolk*. Vice-Admiral Hollands had brought his ship, together with the *Prince of Wales* and six destroyers, at full speed to try and cut the enemy off in the Denmark Strait. All the crews of the ships were put on battle stations shortly after midnight and after five and a half hours of waiting the prey came into sight at 0535. At 0553 firing opened up simultaneously at a range of 25,000 yards, the *Hood* and *Prince of Wales* firing on the *Bismarck* and *Bismarck* and *Prinz Eugen* at once replying. Following discreetly astern, the crews of *Norfolk* and *Suffolk* watched with anticipation; their guns could not cope with the enormous fire power now being used. Could the *Hood* and *Prince of Wales* outgun the pride of the German Navy?

HMS Hood blows up

The first hit went to the *Prinz Eugen* in little under a minute starting a fire on *Hood* which spread rapidly forward and set the whole ship ablaze. The range between the ships was decreasing rapidly and several times the *Bismarck* just missed the *Hood*. Then, suddenly, the British were horror-struck to see a vast flame leap upwards between the *Hood's* masts. A direct hit

had been scored. There was a huge explosion between the after funnel and the main mast and the *Hood* sank within three to four minutes; she had fired only five or six salvos in the whole action. The *Hood* had gone. Only then was it realized what had happened. *Bismarck* had fired a salvo and scored a hit upon *Hood*. The battle cruiser had been struck in the neighbourhood of a magazine. The *Hood*, one of the oldest British warships afloat, had met with sudden and complete destruction. There were to be only 3 survivors out of a total complement of 1,419 officers and men. 44,600 tons of battleship and 1,416 people had been lost at a single stroke.

Now it was the *Prince of Wales'* turn for the enemy's ferocity. So much water was being thrown up around the *Prince of Wales* by exploding shells that onlookers thought that she in turn was doomed. The range was about 18,000 yards. Within a very few minutes she was hit by four 15-inch shells and probably three smaller 8-inch shells. The bridge received a direct hit and instantly became a shambles. Every officer and man on the bridge was killed or wounded except Captain J. C. Leach, the Commanding Officer, and the Chief Yeoman. In the plotting room just below the wrecked bridge, blood began to drip off the end of the bridge voice-pipe onto the plot.

Prince of Wales withdraws

As well as the direct shell damage, small mechanical breakdowns were now seriously affecting the efficiency of the *Prince of Wales*. Captain Leach decided that the time had come to withdraw. Still more shells poured into her, two piercing her side at the waterline and flooding a number of compartments. Captain Leach had moved during the chaos to the lower bridge to command his ship, the wheel was put over and *Prince of Wales* retired from the engagement with all the speed she could muster. In pure arrogance *Bismarck* and *Prinz Eugen* made no attempt to follow but let the wounded ship limp away to lick its wounds. Theirs was the greater prize ahead,

Overleaf Bismarck *engages the 44,600 ton* Hood, *an early victim of the battle. A shell from the German ship struck the* Hood *near the magazine, which exploded. 1,416 men died on the* Hood *and only three survived.*

the rich pickings of the North Atlantic. They thought that now the way was clear, for they had sunk the *Hood*, the best and the biggest warship of the British Fleet, and they had sunk her decisively in a short swift action. The *Bismarck* may have been extremely lucky in penetrating the *Hood's* armour to explode her the way she did, but the fact remains that the *Hood* sank after a very short action.

Vice-Admiral Sir James Sommerville received the news of the sinking of *Hood* and the damage to the *Prince of Wales* with some dismay. Force H, which was under his command, consisted of the battle cruiser *Renown*, the aircraft carrier *Ark Royal*, the cruiser *Sheffield* and six destroyers, was stationed at Gibraltar, 1,500 miles away. Its normal duty had been to seal the western exit of the Mediterranean – now it was decided to throw Force H into play against *Bismarck*.

The *Bismarck*, too, had suffered injury in the action. Three times she had been hit, a glancing blow across the deck, one just forward of the port boiler room, this immobilizing one of her main dynamos, and a shell which passed through her bows, piercing two oil tanks. It was this shot that

eventually sealed her fate. At the time the loss of oil was considered quite insignificant, for still the greater prizes of the North Atlantic lured the *Bismarck* and *Prinz Eugen* on. These three bruises were nothing compared to the pride they felt after sinking one capital ship and damaging another.

Keeping in touch

Norfolk and *Suffolk* had gone on shadowing after the *Hood* was sunk. After some hours the weather cleared and the cruisers kept the *Bismarck* and the *Prinz Eugen* at a range of 15 to 18 miles. At 1100, however, the weather quickly deteriorated, mist rising rapidly. The cruisers closed in as much as they dared but about noon they lost sight and radar contact became intermittent. Shadowing continued until at 1830 *Suffolk* reported that the range by radar was rapidly decreasing. Captain Ellis was alert against such an ambush, he turned the ship hard away and increased to full speed. *Bismarck* was now on the *Suffolk's* port quarter and opening fire at long range. A few salvos were

Opposite above Hood *at anchor in Scapa Flow. Built in 1911, she was Britain's oldest warship.*

Above Hood *explodes – a shell hit her magazine.* Prince of Wales, *to the left, looks on.*

exchanged. The brief action took both ships towards the *Norfolk* and *Prince of Wales*. The *Prince of Wales* opened fire in support of *Suffolk* and *Bismarck* turned away.

This rather aimless ploy of the *Bismarck* – going into action again so quickly – was a cover for what was really happening. During the early afternoon, Admiral Lutjens had decided *Prinz Eugen* was to carry out warfare independently in the North Atlantic while the *Bismarck* was to make full speed for one of the ports on the Biscay coast so that the slight damage to the oil tanks might be repaired. Then she could join the *Prinz Eugen* in their plunderings.

Lutjens now hoped to shake off his pursuers, but they clung more desperately than ever to his tail worried lest by a sudden increase of speed the *Bismarck* might give them the slip and realizing that the only way to prevent this was to launch attack after attack as quickly and as often as possible in order to maim the prey.

Aircraft attack

The first way this could be done, in fact the only way at this particular point, was for the aircraft from HMS *Victorious* to enter the attack and so, for the first time in the history of naval warfare, a battleship at sea was attacked by aircraft launched from their mother carrier. Number 825 Squadron, stationed on *Victorious*, of the Fleet Air Arm consisted of nine Fairey Swordfish bi-planes and six Fulmar monoplanes but unprepared as it was, only nine aircraft could be made ready in haste to be launched against the might of the Bismarck. Each of the seven Swordfish and the two Fulmars were armed with one deadly torpedo.

The untrained flight crews gallantly pressed home their attack, all the torpedoes being dropped – but only one was seen to strike the ship. The single hit was on the *Bismarck* amidships. All the

Above Sheffield, *one of the ships that shadowed the* Bismarck. *She had the misfortune to be attacked by British aircraft who mistook her for the German ship but fortunately was not damaged.*

Below Bismarck, *under attack, fires a salvo from her 15-inch guns. She had eight such guns as well as 12 5·9-inch guns, 16 4·1-inch and 16 20mm anti-aircraft guns.*

Swordfish aircraft returned to the *Victorious* and landed successfully. The two Fulmars stayed in the air, shadowing the prey.

So the day ended, the pursuers demoralized and annoyed for they had suffered heavily, and *Bismarck*, the object of their hoped-for revenge, appeared to be slipping slowly but surely away from them. The escorting destroyers had had to break off for the long high-speed pursuit had run their fuel levels dangerously low for them to remain in the chase. The bruised *Prince of Wales*, the *Norfolk* and *Suffolk*, continued to follow the *Bismarck* throughout that night, reporting her course and speed, at intervals, to the Commander in Chief.

Where is the Bismarck?

Still the *Bismarck* played with her pursuers. At about 0100 on May 25, she mockingly exchanged shots with the *Prince of Wales* at maximum range.

All the shells fell wide. Although this was a somewhat pointless gesture it had the effect of making the *Suffolk*'s shadowing even more difficult. The *Suffolk* was on extreme radar range and at the same time zig-zagging to avoid U-boats which were believed to be in the area. But worse fortune was to befall the pursuers. At 0306 on May 25 at a nominal radar range of 20,900 yards she lost contact with the *Bismarck* through a mixture of bad luck and over confidence. The enemy had altered course sharply to starboard while the *Suffolk* was moving to port and by the time the *Suffolk* returned on the dog leg of the zig-zag the *Bismarck* had gone. She was to stay lost for $31\frac{1}{2}$ hours.

Where was the *Bismarck*? What was her course? Had the killer of the mighty *Hood* escaped? *Suffolk* searched towards the enemy's last bearing during the morning of May 25 but it became obvious that the enemy had evaded her pursuers. Aircraft from *Victorious* were put into action this time to search, but the attempt proved

negative. *Norfolk* and *Suffolk* had searched to the south-east of the last reported position but they too drew a blank. There was no sign of *Bismarck*, she had gone. Then came a stroke of luck – at 1030 on May 26 a Royal Air Force Catalina Flying Boat of Coastal Command, flying on patrol, sighted the *Bismarck*. The hunt was on again. Within a few minutes of the Catalina sighting, the *Ark Royal*, together with Force H, drew close to the reported position. This time they would never lose sight of her until full vengeance had been extracted. The *Bismarck* had to be pegged back, she had crept a lead of over 50 miles and if this increase were to continue, she would soon be within German bomber range and therefore become almost untouchable. She must, above all else be stopped – the prey could not be allowed to slide from their grasp again.

A British error

The only real hope lay in the *Ark Royal*'s aircraft. A force of 15 Swordfish aircraft flew off at 1450 to strike at the *Bismarck*. The weather was particularly bad in the vicinity of the target, but the crews had been told that no other ship was anywhere nearby. Meanwhile, Vice-Admiral Sommerville had ordered the cruiser *Sheffield* to find and shadow the *Bismarck*. The order was flashed by signal searchlight and went only to the *Sheffield*; the *Ark Royal* never noticed her departure. The flying crews in the rain and mist and virtually nil visibility, picked up a ship on their radar in roughly the expected position. Assuming it to be the *Bismarck* they pressed home their attack – on the *Sheffield*.

Eleven torpedoes were fired at the *Sheffield* – two exploded on hitting the water, three more exploded when crossing the wake of the cruiser and the remainder were successfully avoided by the *Sheffield*. With great forebearance she did not fire a single round in reply!

Luck, however, was now swinging away from the *Bismarck*, the hunted, and towards the Royal Navy, the hunters. A second striking force of 15 aircraft was launched at 1915. Because the number of serviceable aircraft was limited, most of the aircraft which had flown in the first misplaced attack were re-armed and refuelled for the second attack. Heavy rain swept across the flight deck as the planes took off. The feeling on *Ark Royal* was that this striking force must succeed – it was the last chance. This time the Swordfish found their true prey and the attack was pressed home.

Bismarck at bay

In face of intense and accurate fire from *Bismarck* the aircraft swung in pairs and attacked with gallantry and determination. At least two hits were scored on the *Bismarck*, one damaged the rudders and this was to be the Achilles heel. When the aircraft returned five had been severely damaged by gunfire. In one, 127 holes were counted, the pilot and the gunner having both been wounded, but despite all this only one aircraft crashed.

Reports now poured in from the other pursuers that *Bismarck* had drastically altered course. Why was she behaving so strangely? The damage to the rudders must be serious. Straggling aircraft landing on the *Ark Royal* reported that immediately after the attack *Bismarck*, trailing oil, had made two complete circles and apparently come to a stop heading north. She was lying wallowing in the seas. One of the two hits, the one which damaged the rudders, had been so accurate that the steering mechanisms had been virtually destroyed.

The Royal Navy, who had suffered much, now knew their chance was coming. *Bismarck* was lying helpless. The pursuers gathered their strength for the final confrontation, but *Bismarck* was not done yet and she fired six accurate salvos at her persistent chasers as if in defiance to try and keep alive her hopes. The escorting destroyers *Cossack*, *Maori*, *Sikh* and *Zulu* together with the Polish destroyer *Piorun* approached the stricken *Bismarck* and started to harass the enemy. Soon it was clear that the destroyers' main objective was to keep in touch with the enemy and the secondary objective to attack if an opportunity arose. Orders were therefore despatched that the destroyers were to attack independently as opportunity offered and not to risk their ships. Throughout the night and until 0845 on May 27 when the main battle fleet gathered, these destroyers maintained constant touch in spite of heavy rain squalls and low visibility.

The final kill

At 0847 the mighty warships *Rodney* and *King*

George V moved into action. *Rodney*, a 33,900 ton battleship, built in 1925, opened the account with a salvo from her nine 16-inch guns. This was immediately followed by a salvo from the ten 14-inch guns from the 2-year-old, 35,000 ton, battleship *King George V*. The *Bismarck* quickly replied. The battle to the death was on. At 0854 the *Norfolk* opened fire at 20,000 yards. At 0904 the cruiser *Dorsetshire* joined in the action. In order to concentrate their fire power, the battleships continued to close on their target, coming in to 3,300 yards. By 1015 the *Bismarck* was a wreck, without a gun firing, on fire fore and aft and wallowing more heavily every moment. Men could be seen jumping overboard, preferring death by drowning to the appalling effects of the fires which were now raging over her decks. *Bismarck*'s masts were down, the funnel had disappeared and smoke and flames were rising from the middle of the ship. But her flag still flew ostentatiously; she remained defiant though powerless. In the midst of her death throes the

vultures moved in for the kill.

Dorsetshire torpedoed the *Bismarck* on both sides at close range. The proud battleship of the Third Reich was now a battered hulk. The torpedoes exploded right under the remains of the bridge; heeling over to port, then turning upside down, the *Bismarck* shuddered and disappeared beneath the waves. The hunters had finally caught their prey.

Longest chase in history

The destruction of the *Bismarck* had been one of the longest chases in naval history. For Grand Admiral Raeder, Exercise Rhine was at an end. What would have happened if his plan had succeeded and *Bismarck*, *Prinz Eugen* and others had broken out into the North Atlantic to run amok amongst the life supporting convoys that were reaching Britain from the Americas? As it was, thanks to the tenacity, the courage, the forbearance of many officers and men of the Royal Navy during the period from May 18 when the *Bismarck* and *Prinz Eugen* sailed from Gdynia to the time *Bismarck* slid beneath the waves on May 27, the convoys were still able to continue their life-supporting efforts. Exercise Rhine had been

Below Aircraft aboard Victorious *await orders to attack the* Bismarck. Victorious *had nine Swordfish biplanes and six Fulmar monoplanes. Only nine, each armed with one torpedo, were ready when the order came.*

Major ships in the *Bismarck* action

BRITISH SHIPS

Hood
(Battle-cruiser)

Tonnage: 44,600
Speed: 32 knots
Armament: 8 15in., 12 5.5in., 8 4in. AA, 24 2in. guns, 4 21in. torpedoes

Prince of Wales
(Battleship)

Tonnage: 35,000
Speed: 32 knots
Armament: 10 14in., 16 5.25in., 4 pom-pom. Carried four aircraft launched by catapault

Norfolk
(Cruiser)

Tonnage: 9,925
Speed: 32.8 knots
Armament: 8 8in., 8 4in. AA, 4 3-pounder, 16 smaller arms, 8 21in. torpedo tubes. Carried one aircraft launched by catapault

Suffolk
(Cruiser)

Tonnage: 10,000
Speed: 31.5 knots
Armament: 8 8in., 8 4in. AA, 20 smaller arms. Carried one aircraft launched by catapault

Dorsetshire
(Cruiser)

Tonnage: 9,975
Speed: 32 knots
Armament: 8 8in., 8 4in. AA, 4 3-pounder, 16 smaller arms, 8 21in. torpedo tubes. Carried one aircraft launched by catapault.

GERMAN SHIPS

Bismarck
(Battleship)

Tonnage: 50,000
Speed: 29 knots
Armament: 8 15in., 12 5.9in., 16 4.1in. AA, 16 20mm guns. Carried two aircraft launched by catapault

Prinz Eugen
(Cruiser)

Tonnage: 17,000
Speed: 32 knots
Armament: 8 8in., 12 4.1in., 12 37mm AA guns. 12 21 in. torpedo tubes. Carried three aircraft launched by catapault

brilliantly conceived but failed hopelessly in its objectives and the convoy lanes, the life lines of Britain, had been kept open.

The battle had been waged by the older ships of the Royal Navy against the faster and more up to date ships of the German Navy. The Germans had expected to make an easy passage to dominance of the seas, but they had not bargained for bulldog-like tenacity. Once the Royal Navy caught the scent of battle then nothing could shake the belief that victory was the only course of action; and victory was achieved.

There were to be many more confrontations between the Navies of Germany and Britain during World War II. Some were great and some were small, but always, from this action onwards, the German Navy respected her enemy. She was not the tired old lady that they had been led to believe. If Germany wanted dominance of the seas it could only be achieved at a terrible cost. Events were to prove that the cost was too great.

Above Bismarck's *huge guns thunder a salvo at the doomed* Hood. *But Britain had her revenge.*

Right *Voyage to oblivion. The course of the battle was mainly a chase with sporadic and ill-coordinated attacks. But at the end* **inset** *the British ships closed in for the kill.*

Death of the Bismarck

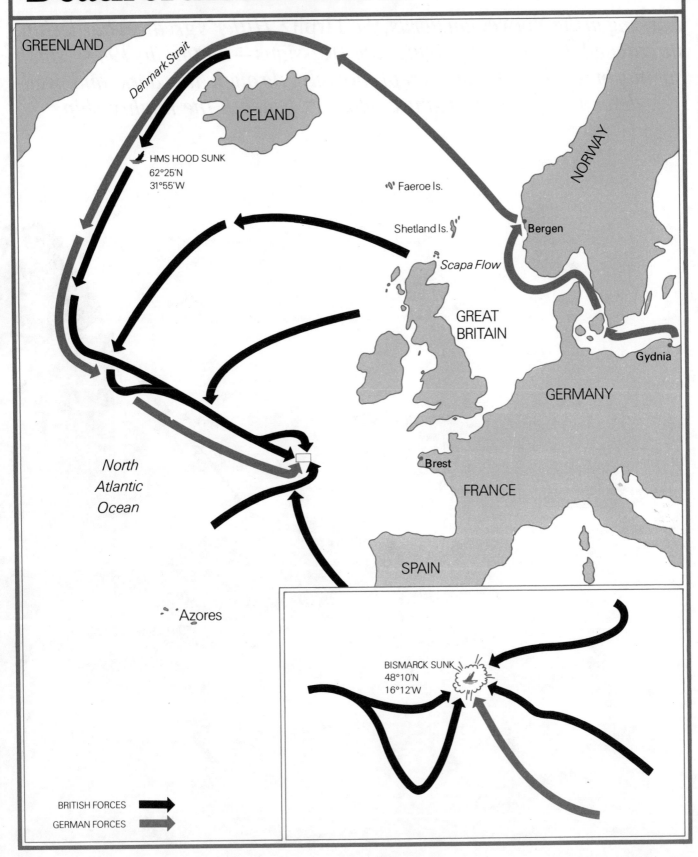

GREENLAND

Denmark Strait

ICELAND

HMS HOOD SUNK
62°25'N
31°55'W

Faeroe Is.

Shetland Is.

Scapa Flow

NORWAY

Bergen

Gydnia

GREAT
BRITAIN

GERMANY

Brest

FRANCE

North
Atlantic
Ocean

Azores

SPAIN

BISMARCK SUNK
48°10'N
16°12'W

BRITISH FORCES

GERMAN FORCES

SUBS v. TIRPITZ

Lurking in the Norwegian fiords, the Tirpitz, *Hitler's greatest battleship, threatened convoys supplying the Russians — until, in 1943, small submarines, the X craft, crept bravely through the dark and well-defended waters to plant explosives beneath the mighty ship.*

Tirpitz, sister ship of the Bismarck, *was a threat to the Russian convoys until severely damaged by bombs laid by X craft, the Allies' midget submarines. Her eight 15-inch guns were never again to fire in action.*

Like minnows in search of a shark, three tiny submarines swam through the hazards of Norway's Altenfiord towards the *Tirpitz,* proud battleship of the German Third Reich. The mission of the submarines was to cripple the mighty fighting ship and prevent her ever again venturing from her icy lair to savage the straggling convoys that were the supplies life line to the hard-pressed Russian ally. The odds were immense – and so was the achievement.

When Russia entered the Second World War in 1941 vast quantities of war materials had to be transported from the embattled Allied forces to the Russian war effort on the Eastern front. The Allies established convoy routes from Great Britain northwards round the North Cape into the White Sea, landing at the Russian port of Archangel.

The Germans had to strangle this life line. They had made the mistake of fighting on two fronts and in both the East and the West the war was taking its toll. But the Russian assault in the East depended on a flow of munitions from the other allies and Hitler and his naval aides soon came to the conclusion that the munitions lifeline, stretching tenuously round the North Cape and into Archangel, must be broken. If the munitions flow could be halted then the sting of Russian aggression on the Eastern front would be blunted, and would eventually cease. So plans already made to move the capital ships of the German Navy into such a position that they could spring out and crush the convoys, were brought into play.

Cats and mice

The plans involved moving the capital ships of the Reich into the naval anchorages of Trondheim, Narvik, and Altenfiord (Altafjord), along the pitted coastline of occupied Norway. These anchorages were natural, deep and winding fiords that cut far into the coastline, dark and dank sanctuaries that were ideal places to hide the capital ships of the German Navy. There the 'cat' would wait, in comparative safety, for the convoys to pass. Then, so the plans had it, the cat could spring from its lair and kill the 'mice', the Allied munitions ships. The munitions lifeline would be severed.

The most northerly and most tortuous harbour chosen by the Third Reich was that at Altenfiord, and here the modern 42,000-ton battleship *Tirpitz* lay. The presence of this warship, the most highly efficient and deadly weapon of the German Navy, played havoc with the already greatly stretched convoys. One convoy, number PQ17, was virtually wiped out after it scattered thinking the *Tirpitz* was out; others were strafed so that very few ships reached their destination, Archangel. If the Russian war effort was to be sustained something had to be done to counter the menace of the predators.

The British Admiralty decided that the only way to safeguard the convoys was the elimination of the German capital ships. But how? Several methods had been tried – all had failed. RAF bombers were sent to blast the ships while at anchor deep in the fiords, but the luck was always with the German Navy. A method to penetrate deep into the fiords, to the very heart of their lairs had to be found.

A new secret weapon

For many months secret trials and practices

The Tirpitz *at anchor in Norway's Altenfiord surrounded by just two of the obstacles the X craft had to overcome – anti-submarine and torpedo nets.*

were carried out on the coast of Scotland, in Loch Scriven, as this was the nearest natural configuration to the fiords of Norway. Here the Royal Navy secretly tested and modified a new weapon, the 'X' craft.

X craft were midget submarines designed to hold four men, and small enough to pick their way stealthily through the many navigational hazards, to negotiate the tortuous and twisting route necessary to avoid minefields and patrol vessels and slip unseen into the battleship's lair. The small submarines were designed to carry a payload of high explosives, two-ton charges which were deployed either side of the craft and could be released by one of the submariners.

A plan of action was devised. The submarines were to enter the guarded anchorage at Alten-fiord and worm their way through the heavy defences to place their lethal explosive under-neath the *Tirpitz*. With the explosive in place the submarines would return by the route by which they came. The plan was ingenious and top secret and in early September 1943, with the trials in Lock Scriven complete, it was designated by an official code-name, 'Operation Source'.

Six Royal Navy midget submarines, HMS X5 to HMS X10 were to enter Altenfiord during the period September 20 to 25. This timing would give them the favourable weather conditions needed. The six X craft, after navigating the fiords, would place their charges under the battleship and leave the fiord.

All was set for Operation Source. Six conventional submarines towed the X craft to their target across the North Sea. But then misfortune struck – two of the midget submarines broke adrift while on passage and were lost. Another developed serious mechanical defects and was forced to abandon the operation. Only three craft were left to enter the predator's lair – the X5, X6, and X7.

First strike

The three midget submarines dived off the entrance to Altenfiord to carry out their task and travelled singly up the tortuous passage. One craft the X6, commanded by Lieutenant Donald Cameron, RNR, suffered mechanical defects; his periscope, the 'eye' of the submarine, was only partly effective. Nevertheless, the X6 was first to strike.

The *Tirpitz* was protected by a very heavy and intricate anti-torpedo net. This encircled her anchorage so that no submerged craft could get within striking distance. It was inpenetrable – or almost. One space had been left open for small

supply boats to ferry men and stores to the great ship. The X6, completely submerged, followed one heavily guarded supply boat through the encircling defensive net and entered the battleship's sanctuary. Before her, immense and threatening, lay the *Tirpitz*. But then disaster struck the brave little predator. While trying to manoeuvre into a position to drop the deadly explosive charges, the X6 smashed into a submerged rock.

Charges in position

The midget submarine was driven almost clear of the water. In the grey half light of morning, the guards on board *Tirpitz* sighted the submarine breaking surface. Though Lt. Cameron managed to regain control it was too late – the alarm had been given. With great courage and fortitude, Cameron brought his damaged submarine close in to the *Tirpitz*, but again disaster struck. Wires hanging over the side of the battleship became entangled with the X6, and for a few moments the midget submarine was trapped. Cameron skilfully managed to extricate his tiny ship and, diving deeper, right under the hull of the *Tirpitz*, he planted his charges.

By now alarm and confusion had spread throughout the Tirpitz at the sighting of the enemy submarine. Lt. Cameron knew the game was up – he could not escape with his damaged submarine. He surfaced close by and abandoned ship. The four submariners were hauled aboard the great warship and the X6 was sent to the bottom of the fiord.

One of the other craft, the X7, commanded by Lieutenant Godfrey Place, RN, had tried to go under the maze of anti-submarine nets. Then at a depth of 75 feet, the craft became entangled in the encircling web. With great skill the commander extricated his vessel and moved silently in on the target. Diving deeper underneath the belly of the mighty battleship Lieutenant Place, too, laid his charges in strategic positions. He turned and began to make his escape but once again the nets snared his ship. The explosive charges had a time fuse – and time was running out fast.

Explosion!

At 0812 hours, some 30 minutes after the charges had been laid, explosions rocked the 42,000 ton *Tirpitz*. Water and steam flew high in the air. Two simultaneous explosions thundered down the fiord, echoing to and fro in a deafening

Opposite The Germans lay smoke screens to hide Tirpitz *from aerial reconnaisance.*

Below The 42,000 ton Tirpitz *carried a crew of 2,400 and included eight 15-inch and 12 5.9 inch guns in her hardware. With a maximum range of 9,000 miles at 19 knots, she posed a fearful threat to the vital convoys.*

crescendo of noise. The *Tirpitz* lurched to one side, a great hole torn below the waterline in her keel. Oil poured from her fuel tanks and spread its slimy fingers over the surface of the water. On board the battleship there was chaos.

The explosions were so violent that the ensnared X7 was blasted clear of the entangling nets and thrust to the surface by the underwater shock waves. German gunners opened fire on the wallowing submarine with small arms, and threw hand grenades to try and sink the fleeing craft. Damage to the X7 was severe and Lt. Place decided to abandon ship. The crew scuttled

Ships in the *Tirpitz* action

Tirpitz (Battleship)		
Launched:	February 14, 1939
Tonnage:	42,900 displacement
Dimensions:	length 823ft. beam 118ft. draught 35ft.
Speed:	29 knots
Armament:	8 15in., 12 5.9in., 16 4.1in., 16 37mm A.A., 70 20mm A.A., 8 21in. torpedo tubes, six aircraft launched from one catapault.
Complement:	2,530

X craft (Submarines)		
Built:	1942-43
Tonnage:	27-30
Speed:	6.5 knots (surface) 5.5 knots (submerged)
Dimensions:	length 51ft. beam 6ft. draught 6ft.
Complement:	4

the brave ship. Tragically only two of the four man crew escaped alive from this daring and courageous exploit.

The third X craft to enter the fiord, the X5, arrived on the scene after the explosion. The Germans, now alert and watchful, spotted her and fired. The X5 was apparently hit and went with her crew to the bottom of the icy waters without delivering a blow to *Tirpitz*.

A most courageous act

In the aftermath of the brave sortie came disappointment. Air-reconnaissance photographs showed the *Tirpitz* still at anchor – it seemed that little damage had been done. What was not known, and would not become apparent for a few months, was that *Tirpitz* had suffered a grievous injury. The hole in her hull had seriously weakened her main structure and her generators and dynamos had been virtually destroyed.

The mighty *Tirpitz* never again ventured out into the Atlantic and never again fired a shot in anger. The small defiant attack by the extremely gallant and courageous crews of the midget submarines had cleared the way for the convoys. The tenuous supply lines could be maintained. Russia received her precious armaments and the war continued against Germany on two major fronts.

It was not until two years after peace that the British public became fully aware of the gallantry of the men in the three tiny submarines. As a reward for the tremendous contribution they had made to the war effort the survivors of Operation Source were proudly presented to, and decorated by, King George VI at Buckingham Palace. An official report by the Admiralty predicted that this 'daring attack will surely go down in history as one of the most courageous acts of all time'.

Above left *The X craft carried a crew of five and had a range of 1,200 miles at 4 knots and at 2 knots could travel submerged for 23 hours. 53 feet long and weighing 30 tons, the X craft carried a warhead of two external charges as well as limpet mines.*

Right *Route of the X craft to the* Tirpitz. ***Inset*** *The convoy route threatened by the German battleship.*

Submarines against Tirpitz

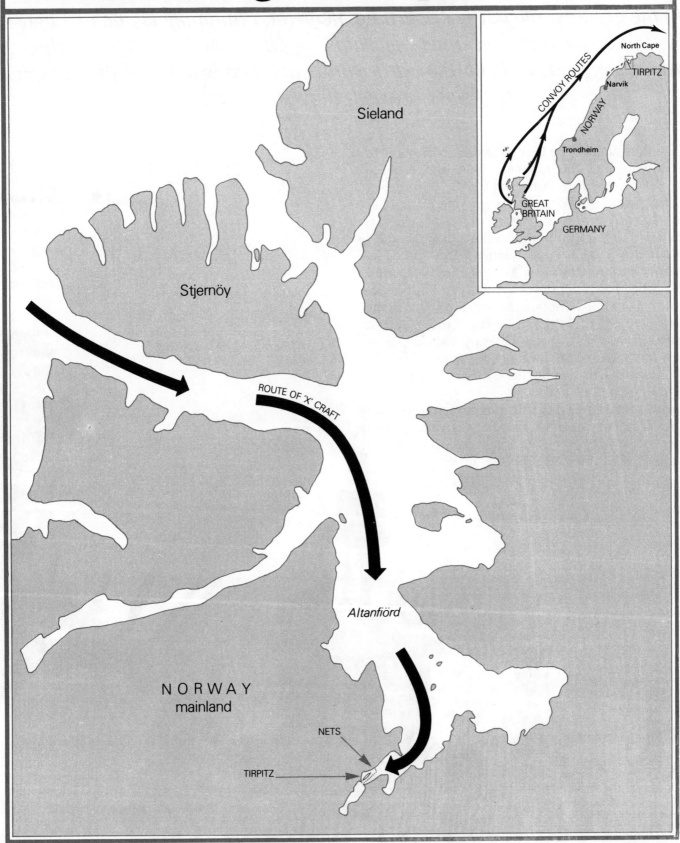

LEYTE GULF

In the greatest sea battle of all time, near the Philippine island of Leyte in 1944, over-matched American ships fought desperately against three Japanese fleets to keep the hard-won beach-heads open. And through bluff and bravery they succeeded.

'The President of the United States ordered me to break through the Japanese lines and proceed from Corregidor to Australia for the purpose, as I understand it, of organizing the American offensive against Japan, a primary object of which is the relief of the Philippines. I came through and I shall return.' Thus spoke General Douglas MacArthur on his arrival in Australia in 1942, after the Allied forces had been virtually run out of the South Pacific by the southward advance of the armed might of Imperial Japan. Little else but Australia was left to the Allies in that theatre of war at that time. It took a bold man indeed to promise to halt the Japanese advance, let alone turn it.

But MacArthur did return, although it was not until October 20, 1944, that he was able to start the northward drive that was to carry him to victory. The build-up to the landings on the

Leyte Gulf, the largest sea battle of modern times was a vital step in America's fight to drive the Japanese from the Philippine Sea and thus sever her oil supply lines from Malaya and Indo-China. By doing this Japan's ability to wage war would be drastically impaired. Here the 33,100 ton Pennsylvania, *which fought at Leyte Gulf, leads an American battle line.*

island of Leyte, in the Philippines, that took place on that day was desperately fought. It was a matter of survival, pure and simple, for the Americans and their numerically weak Australasian allies; for the Japanese it was the final step in their dreams of a Pacific empire.

The last of the preliminary engagements, on June 19 and 20, had been especially costly for the Japanese. In this battle, known officially as the Battle of the Philippines Sea but sometimes irreverently, if accurately, referred to as 'The Great Marianas Turkey Shoot', the Japanese Navy suffered heavy losses. As well as the damage to their ships, they saw the American carrier-

borne aircraft put over 500 of their planes out of action.

The largest sea battle

Both this action and the landings themselves, however, were destined to be no more than a prelude to the battle that followed. It took place in an area of the Philippines known as the Leyte Gulf, and remains the largest sea battle of modern times. Between October 22 and 27, 1944, over 230 warships and 1,996 aircraft took part in this terrible encounter between the forces of the

Far left *Admiral Soemu Toyoda, Commander-in-Chief of the Japanese Combined Fleet.*

Left *'I shall return.' General MacArthur's promise, made in 1942 came true in 1944 when American forces landed in the Philippines.*

Below *American aircraft carriers under attack off Leyte Gulf as seen from the carrier* White Plains.

United States and Imperial Japan. The battle was fought as an adjunct to the invasion of the island of Leyte, the vital stepping-stone in MacArthur's drive to rid the Philippines Sea of Japanese domination. The mighty sea-borne invasion force that he had mustered included no less than 17 aircraft carriers.

The landing on the beaches of Leyte itself, on October 20, met with little opposition, and by the midnight of the following day MacArthur had put ashore 132,000 men. Despite their recent heavy defeats, especially those they suffered during the latter half of June, the Commander of the Japanese Navy, Admiral Suemo Toyoda, was still far from cowed. He was seeking the sea-battle to end all sea-battles, the battle in which he hoped to blunt the American thrust towards Japan.

The Allied plan to land on Leyte was based on the theory that the Philippine archipelago lay directly along the main sea routes from Japan to her sources of oil in Malaya and Indo-China. The operation, to which MacArthur had given the name 'Operation Reno', was designed to cut these sea routes, and thus strangle Japan into surrender, and called on vast concentrations of air, land and sea forces. If these drives into the main life-blood of Japan, her oil routes, could be completed successfully, her ability to wage war would be severely impaired.

MacArthur lands

As soon as the USS *Nashville* had landed General MacArthur and his entourage on Leyte, the General, in his usual dramatic tones, spoke to his troops. Although fighting was still going on with

the Japanese not many yards away, a mobile broadcasting unit was set up and General Mac-Arthur spoke these, now famous, words: 'People of the Philippines; I have returned. By the grace of Almighty God, our forces stand again on Philippine soil, soil consecrated in the blood of our two peoples. We have come, dedicated and committed to the task of destroying every vestige of enemy control over your daily lives, and of restoring upon a foundation of indestructible strength the liberties of your people. . . .

'Rally to me. Let the indomitable spirit of Bataan and Corregidor lead on. As the lines of battle roll forward to bring you within the zone of operations, rise and strike. Strike at every favourable opportunity. For your homes and hearths, strike! For future generations of your sons and daughters, strike! In the name of your sacred dead, strike! Let no heart be faint.

Let every arm be steeled. The guidance of divine God points the way. Follow His name to the Holy Grail of righteous victory.' These words were indeed to bring the fighting spirit of the Philippine people to the surface.

Toyoda's last gamble

The time had come for Admiral Toyoda to make his last decisive gamble. Having heard of the American invasion, he set out from his base in Singapore with every ship he could muster. He

The American aircraft carrier Hornet, *27,000 tons. MacArthur's huge invasion force included no less than 17 carriers, but found itself stretched by the massive Japanese onslaught.*

divided the combined fleet of the Imperial Japanese Navy into three distinct groups: central force under Admiral Kurita, southern force rear group, under Vice Admiral Kiyohide Shima with southern force forward group, under Vice Admiral Nishimura, and northern force, under Vice Admiral Ozawa.

Toyoda's plan was for central force to pass through the San Bernardino Strait, north of Leyte, and then set course southwards for Leyte Gulf. Southern force would approach through the Mindanao Sea and Surigao Strait so that both fleets would converge simultaneously on the flanks of the attacking American naval fleet in a coordinated pincer-attack. Northern force, in the Philippines Sea, was to decoy the powerful United States Third Fleet from its job of protecting the entrance to Leyte Gulf.

The American naval forces involved in the Leyte invasion were disposed in two main bodies. The Seventh Fleet, under Vice Admiral Thomas C. Kinkaid, protected the southern and western entrances to Leyte Gulf, while the stronger Third Fleet, under Admiral Halsey, operated off Samar. It was his task to cover the San Bernardino Strait and the approaches from the north west.

Central force mauled

On October 24 General MacArthur moved his headquarters ashore. The *Nashville*, which had been his headquarters during the landing, moved into its position for the coming battle. During the day, Admiral Kurita's central force was put under constant attack by aircraft from the Third Fleet and could therefore only cautiously edge its way towards the entrance to the San Bernardino Strait. The first blows were falling to the American Navy: the *Musashi*, a new addition to the Imperial Navy, with nine 18.1-inch guns, was sunk. Her sister ship, the *Yamato*, was severely hit. Some Japanese cruisers were also damaged or put out of action, as were some of their smaller destroyers.

At 1553 hours the Japanese staged a temporary withdrawal of their central force, to enable them to regroup their now badly mauled formations. This was completed in less than two hours, and at 1714 hours the central force again advanced. Admiral Toyoda issued the following communique to his forces: 'All forces will dash to the

attack, trusting in divine assistance.' He was determined to crush the American fleet with everything at his disposal.

Southern force ambushed

Meanwhile, the Japanese southern force, the other arm of the proposed pincer movement, was sailing at speed into the Mindanao Sea. The American forces had not been idle either: armed with excellent intelligence reports on the movements of the Japanese ships, they had prepared an ambush in a narrow passage at the entrance to the Surigao Strait with torpedo-boats, destroyers, cruisers and battleships.

The torpedo-boats and destroyers attacked the Japanese ships from both sides as they sailed in line astern formation into the entrance to the narrow strait. The cruisers and battleships, stationed ahead of the Japanese, then joined the action, using their big guns as soon as the Japanese came within range. The ambush was a complete success, and the whole southern force of the Japanese fleet was virtually annihilated. Indeed, this attack was almost perfect for only one Japanese destroyer escaped. The southern entrance to Leyte Gulf was completely cleared of Japanese naval forces in one swift defiant action.

Northern force's bad luck

At this stage only the northern force had made no contact and luck was to play a most important part for the Americans. The Japanese force was continually sending radio messages in order to advertise their position and lure the Americans into an unfavourable battle position. But a fault in their transmission systems prevented the Third Fleet from intercepting and acting on these signals. The American forces never knew of the enticement to fight that was being dangled in front of them! Vice Admiral Ozawa could not wage battle as he wished.

Due to the complete disaster that had befallen the southern force, and the lack of success of the northern force's tactics, the task of destroying a large proportion of the United States Navy now rested solely with Admiral Kurita and the regrouped central force of the Japanese fleet. At dawn on October 25 yet another battle took place.

Battle commences

A group of 16 escort carriers, nine cruisers and 12 destroyers of the Seventh Fleet were disposed east of Samar and the Leyte Gulf, directly in the path of the oncoming Japanese force. The light carriers of the American Navy were no real match for the massive battleships and aircraft carriers of the heavily armed Japanese central force. A battle between completely unequal adversaries commenced but the Americans realized the danger they faced should the Japanese break through and gain entrance to the Leyte Gulf. The powerful battleships, with their huge guns, could lay waste the beach-heads that MacArthur had just recently taken. The Americans planned their tactics accordingly.

At 0658 hours, the battleship *Yamato* fired her huge 18.1-inch guns, and the battle was on. Never before had the American fleet been subjected to such concentrated heavy firepower. In addition to the surface units, Kamikaze or suicide attacks were made on the American carriers by Japanese air units based in the Philippines. The central force continued to press home their attack, at

The American battleship Texas, *27,000-tons. Her main armament consisted of ten 14-inch guns. Two Japanese battleships carried 18.1-inch guns.*

full speed. But the American fleet was not to be battered into submission quite so easily.

Battleships versus carriers

A brilliant display of co-ordinated counter-thrusts then took place. No sooner had Yamato's shells been fired than aircraft were launched from the American escort carriers, and the orders were to destroy or cripple the big guns as quickly as possible. The situation was rapidly reaching a critical point for both sides. The American fleet laid smoke screens – and used every tactical trick in the book: central force had to be stopped in its tracks by the weaker American fleet. The beach-heads must be protected at all cost.

The destroyer escorts were sent in to harry the enormous, and therefore slightly cumbersome Japanese battleships. Although they took heavy punishment, they pressed home their attack like dogs barking at the heels of a great dragon and started to inflict small but telling wounds on the mighty warships. Aircraft buzzed like hornets around the dragon's head, continually attacking and thrusting. But American ships were being put out of action and sunk and the battleships of the Imperial Japanese Navy thundered on. They were creating havoc amongst the American forces by now, their heavy firepower damaging the cruisers and destroyers severely. Kamikaze aircraft had smashed open the flight decks of the aircraft carriers, so that the returning planes had nowhere to land. Some were able to make for the sanctuary of the airstrip at Tacloban, but others, who had carried the battle to the limits of their range, and had expected to be able to return to their mother carriers, were compelled to ditch in Leyte Gulf.

Disaster now stared the Americans in the face. At 0900 hours the American forces issued this signal: 'Our escort carriers being attacked by four battleships, eight cruisers plus others. Request fast carriers make immediate strike.' Help was wanted quickly or they would perish, and already the American losses had started to mount alarmingly. After two and a half hours of continuous battle their ammunition was running

Left Japanese ships in the Tablas Strait take evasive action during an attack by American aircraft during the battle of Leyte Gulf.

low, their destroyers had expanded all their torpedoes and their planes had to be refuelled and rearmed many miles away.

Victory for Japan?

Victory lay within the Imperial Japanese Navy's grasp – but could they close their fingers and grip it? This was the desperate question passing through the minds of the men of the United States Navy. Then suddenly, the impossible happened. Inexplicably the Imperial Japanese Navy turned away: their units had sustained more damage than had been, at first glance, apparent and believing that the American forces were falling back in order to muster another attack, they retreated.

To the US carriers, this was a blessing for they had been receiving a terrible pounding, now instead of the Japanese advantage being forced home, they were being let off the hook. The American carrier forces and their destroyer escorts set up a huge smoke-screen behind which they, too, retreated to regroup.

The Japanese withdrawal lasted until 1120 hours when, after regrouping and making some quick repairs, the remains of the central force mounted one last attempt on Leyte Gulf. But fate again stepped in: unsure of their own strength, the Japanese commanders hesitated. Their central force was less than one hour from its objective, but their uncertainty made them

Above American patrol boats were used for spotting and attacking Japanese forces and for rescuing survivors. A cameraman on board the USS Hancock pictures crewmen of PT 321 fishing a Japanese sailor out of the water.

Right the scene of the Battle of Leyte Gulf and the positions of the contending fleets. Inset shows the position of the Philippines in the China Sea.

give up this last attempt. They turned round at 1236 hours, one hour and sixteen minutes after attempting their final assault in a mood of indecision that finally culminated in a complete withdrawal. The central force passed back out through the San Bernardino Strait, and by 2130 hours on October 25 the remains of the Japanese navy were scurrying home.

American bluff–and courage

The Seventh Fleet had held out despite a tremendous hammering and against almost overwhelming odds. In the end, by a good deal of bluff, they had persuaded the enemy that they were stronger than they really were. Thus the battle of Leyte Gulf drew to a close, with the Japanese navy completely routed.

When the engagement finished with small skirmishes on October 27, the toll against the Imperial Japanese Navy had been heavy. Of the 65 ships that started, 26 had been sunk, including

Leyte Gulf

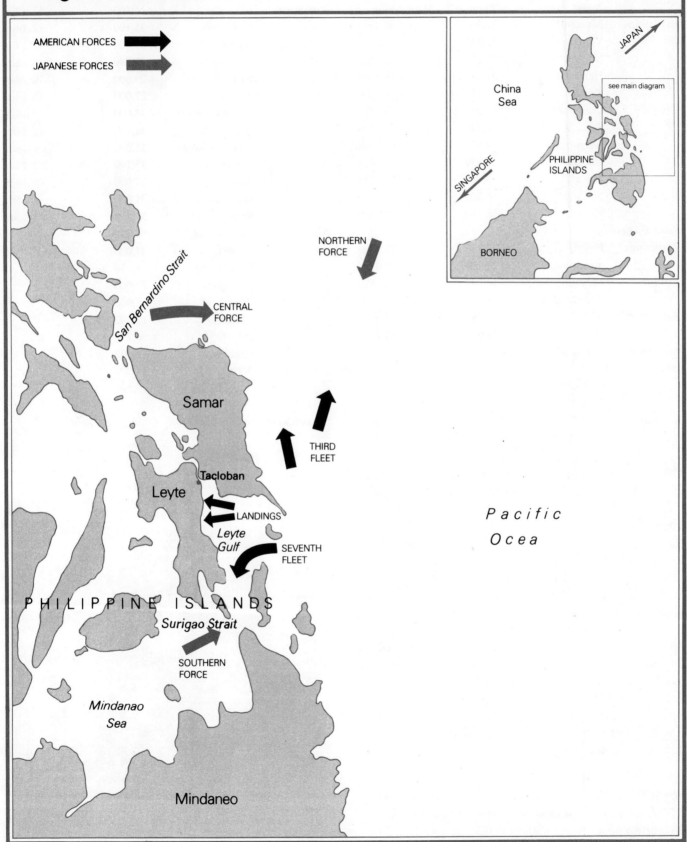

AMERICAN FORCES

JAPANESE FORCES

China
Sea

JAPAN

see main diagram

PHILIPPINE
ISLANDS

SINGAPORE

BORNEO

NORTHERN
FORCE

San Bernardino Strait

CENTRAL
FORCE

Samar

THIRD
FLEET

Tacloban

Leyte

LANDINGS

Leyte
Gulf

SEVENTH
FLEET

P a c i f i c

O c e a

P H I L I P P I N E   I S L A N D S

Surigao Strait

SOUTHERN
FORCE

Mindanao
Sea

Mindaneo

Major ships in the Battle of Leyte Gulf

JAPANESE FLEET:

Central Force

	Name	Tonnage	Main Armament
Battleships	Musashi*	42,500	9 16in.
	Yamato	42,500	9 16in.
	Nagato	32,720	8 16in.
	Haruna	29,330	8 14in.
	Kongo	29,330	8 14in.
Cruisers	Chikuma*	14,000	8 8in.
	Suzuya*	14,000	8 8in.
	Atago*	9,850	10 8in.
	Chokai*	9,850	10 8in.
	Maya*	9,850	10 8in.
	Noshiro	6,000	6 6.1in.
	Kinu	5,170	7 5.5in.

Southern Force

	Name	Tonnage	Main Armament
Battleships	Fuso*	29,330	12 14in.
	Yamashiro*	29,330	12 14in.
Cruisers	Mogami*	14,000	8 8in.

'Northern Force'

	Name	Tonnage	Main Armament
Battleships	Ise	29,990	12 14in.
	Hyuga	29,990	12 14in.
Aircraft carriers	Zuikaku*	29,800	
	Zuiho*	12,000	
	Chitose*	9,000	
	Chiyoda*	9,000	
Cruisers	Tama*	5,100	7 5.5in.

AMERICAN FLEET:

	Name	Tonnage	Main Armament
Battleships	Arkansas	26,100	12 12in.
	California	35,190	12 14in.
	Idaho	33,400	12 14in.
	Maryland	33,590	8 16in.
	Nevada	29,000	10 14in.
	New York	27,000	10 14in.
	North Carolina	35,000	9 16in.
	Pennsylvania	33,100	12 14in.
	South Dakota	35,000	9 16in.
	Tennessee	35,190	12 14in.
	Texas	27,000	10 14in.
	Washington	35,000	9 16in.
	West Virginia	33,590	8 16in.
Aircraft carriers	Gambier Bay*	6,730	
	Hornet	27,000	
	Kitkum Bay	6,730	
	Lexington	27,000	
	Princeton*	11,000	
	Santee	12,000	
	St Lo*	6,730	
	Suwanee	12,000	
	Wasp	27,000	
	White Plains	6,730	

Vessels known to have been sunk

the entire force of Japanese carriers, three battleships, and ten cruisers. Even the flagship *Musashi* had gone down. For the sinking of these 26 ships the United States Navy had lost six capital ships out of a total of 166. The six ships sunk included a light aircraft carrier and some small carriers and destroyers. Four days of hard battle had ended in a Japanese defeat of great magnitude.

General MacArthur was naturally delighted that the American navy had managed to protect his landing. He sent this signal: 'At this time I wish to express to you and to all elements of your fine command my deep appreciation of the splendid service they have rendered in the recent Leyte operations. . . . We could not have gone along without them.'

Right *The 11,000 ton aircraft carrier* Princeton *explodes. Fire caused by a bomb had reached the magazine. The* Princeton *sank.*